# MEETING LIFE

## By J. Krishnamurti

# Meeting Life

## Writings and Talks on Finding Your Path Without Retreating from Society

### J. Krishnamurti

HarperSanFrancisco
*A Division of HarperCollinsPublishers*

FIRST EDITION

Krishnamurti, J. (Jiddu).
    Meeting life : writings and talks on finding your path without retreating from society / J. Krishnamurti. — 1st ed.
        p.   cm.
    ISBN 0-06-250526-2 (alk. paper)
    1. Philosophy.    2. Conduct of life.    I. Title.
B6134.K754A5    1991
181'.4—dc20                                                    90-55785
                                                                   CIP

01            RRD-H  12

This edition is printed on acid-free paper that meets the American National Standards Institute Z39.48 Standard.

# Contents

# Introductory Note

The contents of this book are taken from the Krishnamurti Foundation Bulletins. The great majority of items were first published in the Bulletin of the Krishnamurti Foundation Trust in England, a few originally appeared in the Indian and American Bulletins, and then were reprinted in the English Bulletin. Issue numbers referred to are those of the English Bulletin.

The book has been divided into three parts. PART I consists of sixteen short pieces dictated by Krishnamurti. All but three of them are undated; they have therefore been arranged in the order in which they appeared in the Bulletins. This part also includes three longer, dated pieces written by Krishnamurti.

PART II contains Krishnamurti's answers to questions put to him at the end of his talks or at small discussions. Since these are dated, except for two, they appear chronologically, irrespective of the dates of the Bulletins in which they were published.

PART III consists of talks by Krishnamurti in Switzerland, India, England and California. These, also being dated, have been placed chronologically.

# PART I

# *Short Pieces*

# The Lake

The lake was very deep, with soaring cliffs on both sides. You could see the other shore, wooded, with new spring leaves; and that side of the lake was steeper, perhaps more dense with foliage, and heavily wooded. The water was placid that morning and its colour was blue-green. It is a beautiful lake. There were swans, ducks and an occasional boat with passengers.

As you stood on the bank, in a well-kept park, you were very close to the water. It was not polluted at all, and its texture and beauty seemed to enter into you. You could smell it – the soft fragrant air, the green lawn – and you felt one with it, moving with the slow current, the reflections, and the deep quietness of the water.

The strange thing was that you felt such a great sense of affection, not for anything or for anyone, but the fullness of what may be called love. The only thing that matters is to probe into the very depth of it, not with the silly little mind with its endless mutterings of thought, but with silence. Silence is the only means, or instrument, that can penetrate into something that escapes the mind which is so contaminated.

We do not know what love is. We know the symptoms of it, the pleasure, the pain, the fear, the anxiety and so on. We try to solve the symptoms, which becomes a wandering in darkness. We spend our days and nights in this, and it is soon over in death.

There, as you were standing on the bank watching the beauty of the water, all human problems and institutions, man's relationship to man, which is society – all would find their right place if silently you could penetrate into this thing called love.

We have talked a great deal about it. Every young man says he loves some woman, the priest his god, the mother her children, and of course the politician plays with it. We have really spoilt the word and loaded it with meaningless substance – the substance of our own narrow little selves. In this narrow little context we try to find the other thing, and painfully return to our everyday confusion and misery.

But there it was, on the water, all about you, in the leaf, and in the duck that was trying to swallow a large piece of bread, in the lame woman who went by. It was not a romantic identification or a cunning rationalized verbalization. But it was there, as factual as that car, or that boat.

It is the only thing which will give an answer to all our problems. No, not an answer, for then there will be no problems. We have problems of every description and we try to solve them without that love, and so they multiply and grow. There is no way to approach it, or to hold it, but sometimes, if you will stand by the roadside, or by the lake, watching a flower or a tree, or the farmer tilling his soil, and if you are silent, not dreaming, not collecting day-dreams, or weary, but with silence in its intensity, then perhaps it will come to you.

When it comes, do not hold it, do not treasure it as an experience. Once it touches you, you will never be the same again. Let that operate, and not your greed, your anger or your righteous social indignation. It is really quite wild, untamed, and its beauty is not respectable at all.

But we never want it, for we have a feeling that it might be too dangerous. We are domesticated animals, revolving in a cage which we have built for ourselves – with its contentions, wranglings, its impossible political leaders, its gurus who exploit our self-conceit and their own with great refinement or rather crudely. In the cage you can have anarchy or order, which in turn gives way to disorder; and this has been going on for many centuries – exploding, and falling back, changing the patterns of the social structure,

4

perhaps ending poverty here or there. But if you place all these as the most essential, then you will miss the other.

Be alone sometimes, and if you are lucky it might come to you, on a falling leaf, or from that distant solitary tree in an empty field.

*From* BULLETIN I, 1968

## *To Die to Every Yesterday*

Death is only for those who have, and for those who have a resting-place. Life is a movement in relationship and attachment; the denial of this movement is death. Have no shelter outwardly or inwardly; have a room, or a house, or a family, but don't let it become a hiding-place, an escape from yourself.

The safe harbour which your mind has made in cultivating virtue, in the superstition of belief, in cunning capacity or in activity, will inevitably bring death. You can't escape from death if you belong to this world, to the society of which you are. The man who died next door or a thousand miles away is you. He has been preparing for years with great care to die, like you. Like you he called living a strife, a misery, or a jolly good show. But death is always there watching, waiting. But the one who dies each day is beyond death.

To die is to love. The beauty of love is not in past remembrances or in the images of tomorrow. Love has no past and no future; what has, is memory, which is not love. Love with its passion is just beyond the range of society, which is you. Die, and it is there.

Meditation is a movement in and of the unknown. You are not there, only the movement. You are too petty or too

5

great for this movement. It has nothing behind it or in front of it. It is that energy which thought-matter cannot touch. Thought is perversion for it is the product of yesterday; it is caught in the toils of centuries and so it is confused, unclear. Do what you will, the known cannot reach out for the unknown. Meditation is the dying to the known.

Out of silence look and listen. Silence is not the ending of noise; the incessant clamour of the mind and heart does not end in silence; it is not a product, a result of desire, nor is it put together by will. The whole of consciousness is a restless, noisy movement within the borders of its own making. Within this border silence or stillness is but the momentary ending of the chatter; it is the silence touched by time. Time is memory and to it silence is short or long; it can measure. Give to it space and continuity, and then it becomes another toy. But this is not silence. Everything put together by thought is within the area of noise, and thought in no way can make itself still. It can build an image of silence and conform to it, worshipping it, as it does with so many other images it has made, but its formula of silence is the very negation of it; its symbols are the very denial of reality. Thought itself must be still for silence to be. Silence is always now, as thought is not. Thought, always being old, cannot possibly enter into that silence which is always new. The new becomes the old when thought touches it. Out of this silence, look and talk. The true anonymity is out of this silence and there is no other humility. The vain are always vain, though they put on the garment of humility, which makes them harsh and brittle. But out of this silence the word 'love' has a wholly different meaning. This silence is not out there but it is where the noise of the total observer is not.

Innocence alone can be passionate. The innocent have no sorrow, no suffering, though they have had a thousand experiences. It is not the experiences that corrupt the mind but what they leave behind, the residue, the scars, the memories. These accumulate, pile up one on top of the other, and then sorrow begins. This sorrow is time. Where time is, innocency is not. Passion is not born of sorrow. Sorrow is experience, the experience of everyday life, the life of agony and fleeting pleasures, fears and certainties. You cannot escape from experiences, but they need not take root in the soil of the mind. These roots give rise to problems, conflicts and constant struggle. There is no way out of this but to die each day to every yesterday. The clear mind alone can be passionate. Without passion you cannot see the breeze among the leaves or the sunlight on the water. Without passion there is no love.

Seeing is the doing. The interval between seeing and doing is the waste of energy.

Love can only be when thought is still. This stillness can in no way be manufactured by thought. Thought can only put together images, formulas, ideas, but this stillness can never be touched by thought. Thought is always old, but love is not.

The physical organism has its own intelligence, which is made dull through habits of pleasure. These habits destroy the sensitivity of the organism, and this lack of sensitivity makes the mind dull. Such a mind may be alert in a narrow and limited direction and yet be insensitive. The depth of such a mind is measurable and is caught by images and illusions. Its very superficiality is its only brightness. A light and intelligent organism is necessary for meditation. The interrelationship between the meditative mind and its organism is a constant adjustment in sensitivity; for meditation needs freedom. Freedom is its own discipline. In freedom alone can there be attention. To be aware of inattention is to be attentive. Complete attention is love. It alone can see, and the seeing is the doing.

Desire and pleasure end in sorrow; and love has no sorrow. What has sorrow is thought – thought which gives continuity to pleasure. Thought nourishes pleasure, giving strength to it. Thought is everlastingly seeking pleasure, and so inviting pain. The virtue which thought cultivates is the way of pleasure and in it there is effort and achievement. The flowering of goodness is not in the soil of thought but in freedom from sorrow. The ending of sorrow is love.

*From* BULLETIN 4, 1969

## The Garden

It was a very large garden of several acres just outside a sprawling town in the suburbs. There were very large trees and deep shadows – tamarind trees, mangoes, palms and flowering trees. There was colour everywhere, and a pond with lilies in it. And there were newly planted seedlings that would grow into great towering trees. The garden was surrounded by broken barbed wire and one had to chase out goats that wandered in and, occasionally, a cow or two.

The house was large, not too convenient and the room overlooked a lawn which needed watering twice a day, for the sun was too strong for the tender grass. And there were always birds – parrots, minahs, tits, crows, and a large speckled bird with a long tail which used to come and pick at the berries, and a very bright yellow bird which would flash in and out among the leaves.

It was quiet in that garden, but every morning around half past four there would be singing, radios blaring from across the river and snatches of chanting in Sanskrit – because it was a festive month. This chanting was beautiful, but the rest of the music was rather trying. One afternoon, a few hundred yards away in the poor quarter, they were playing a gramophone with cinema music, turned on as loudly as possible. It went on until the evening; it reached the climax at about nine o'clock.

There was a political rally and there were neon lights blazing and a political speaker was holding forth. Apparently he was promising the most extravagant things. He was as fickle as the audience, who would vote according to their fancies. It was really an entertainment, lasting for several hours.

Again in the early morning the religious music would begin; you saw the Southern Cross over the palm trees: and there was silence on the land.

The politician was seeking power for his party through himself. The desire to dominate, to compel and to be obeyed seems so close to man. You see this in a small child and in a so-called mature man – with all its subtlety, cruelty and ugliness. The dictators, the priests and the head of the family, whether it be a man or a woman, seem to demand this obedience. They assume the authority which they have usurped or have been given by tradition, or which they have because they happen to be older. Everywhere this pattern is repeated.

To possess and to be possessed is to give in to this structure of power. This desire for power, position and prestige is encouraged from childhood through comparison and measurement. From this springs conflict, the struggle to achieve, to become a success and to fulfil. And the man who comes with so much respect is showing disrespect to others. The executive with his big car receives respect, and he, in his turn, has great respect for the bigger car, the bigger house, the bigger income.

It is the same in the religious structure of priesthood and also in the hierarchy of gods. Revolutions try to break this down but the same pattern is soon repeated with the dictators on top. The showing of humility becomes an ugly thing in this way of life.

Obedience is violence, and humility is not related to violence. Why should a human being have this fear, respect and disrespect? He is afraid of life with all its uncertainties

9

and anxieties, and he is afraid of the gods of his own mind. It is the fear that leads to power and to aggression.

The intellect is aware of this fear but does nothing about it, and so it builds a society, a church, where this fear is nourished and sustained, with its many escapes. Fear cannot be overcome by thought, for thought has bred fear. Only when thought is silent is there a possibility of fear coming to an end. The man who has power and is competitive obviously does not have love, though he may have a family and children whom he claims to love.

It is really a world of great sorrow, and one must be an outsider to love. To be an outsider is to be alone, uncommitted.

*From* BULLETIN 5, 1970

# The Problem of Living

## MALIBU, CALIFORNIA, 3 MARCH 1970

The mountains were full of solitude. It had been raining off and on for several days and the mountains were green with light. They had become almost blue, and in their fullness they were making the heavens rich and beautiful. There was great silence, which was almost like the sound of the breakers when you walked on the beach over the wet sand. Near the ocean there was no silence except in your heart, but among the mountains, on that winding path, silence was everywhere. The noise of the town, the roar of the traffic and the thunder of waves couldn't be heard.

One is always puzzled about action, and it gets more and more bewildering when one sees the complexity of life.

There are so many things that should be done and there are things that need immediate action. The world around us is changing rapidly – its values, its morality, its wars and peace. One is utterly lost before the immediacy of action. But yet one is always asking oneself what one should do confronted with the enormous problem of living. One has lost faith in most things – in the leaders, in the teachers, in beliefs – and one often wishes there were some clear principle that would light a path, or an authority to tell one what to do. But we know in our hearts that this would be something dead and gone. Invariably we come back to asking ourselves what it is all about and what we must do.

As one can observe, we have always acted from a centre – a centre which contracts and expands. Sometimes it is a very small circle and at other times it is comprehensive, exclusive and utterly satisfying. But it is always a centre of grief and sorrow, of fleeting joys and misery, the enchanting or the painful past. It is a centre which most of us know consciously or unconsciously, and from this centre we act and have our roots. The question of what to do, now or tomorrow, is always asked from the centre and the reply must always be recognizable by the centre. Having received the reply either from another or from ourselves, we proceed to act according to the limitation of the centre. It is like an animal tethered to a post, its action depending on the length of the tether. This action is never free and so there is always pain, mischief and confusion.

Realizing this, the centre says to itself: how am I to be free, free to live happily, completely, openly, and act without sorrow or remorse? But it is still the centre asking the question. The centre is the past. The centre is the 'me' with its selfish activities which knows action only in terms of reward and punishment, achievement or failure, and its motives, causes and effects. It is caught in this chain and the chain is the centre and the prison.

There is another action which comes when there is a

space without a centre, a dimension in which there is no cause and effect. From this, living is action. Here, having no centre, whatever is done is free, joyous, without pain or pleasure. This space and freedom is not a result of effort and achievement, but when the centre ends the other is.

But we will ask how can the centre end, what am I to do to end it, what disciplines, what sacrifices, what great efforts am I to make? None. Only see without choice the activities of the centre, not as an observer, not as an outsider looking inward, but just observe without the censor. Then you may say: I cannot do it, I am always looking with the eyes of the past. Be aware, then, of looking with the eyes of the past, and remain with that. Don't try to do anything about it; be simple and know that whatever you try to do will only strengthen the centre and is a response of your own desire to escape.

So there is no escape, no effort and no despair. Then you can see the full meaning of the centre and the immense danger of it, and that is enough.

*From* BULLETIN 6, 1970

## The Oak Tree

The oak tree that morning was very quiet. It was an enormous tree in the wood; it had a huge trunk and its branches were well above the ground, spread out in all directions – quiet, stable and immovable. It was part of the earth like the other trees that surrounded it. The others would be shouting with the wind, playing with it, and every leaf would belong to the wind. The small leaves of the oak tree played with it too, but there was great dignity and a depth of life that you felt as you watched. Ivy was clinging to many of the trees, going right up to the top of the highest branches, but the oak tree had none of it. Even the pines had this clinging ivy, which, if allowed, would destroy them. And there in that grove were seven or eight tall and massive redwoods which must have been planted centuries ago. They were surrounded by rhododendrons, and in the springtime the grove was a sanctuary not only for birds and rabbits, pheasants and small animals, but also for human beings who cared to go there. You could sit by the hour quietly with the daffodils and the azaleas and look at the blue sky through the leaves. It was an enchanting place and all these massive trees were your friends, if you wanted friends.

It was a place of rare beauty, quiet, isolated, and people hadn't spoilt it. It is strange how human beings desecrate nature with their killing, with their noise and vulgarity. But here, with the redwoods and the oak and all the spring flowers, it was really a sanctuary for the quiet mind, for a mind that is as stable and firm as those trees – not from some belief, some dogma or in some dedicated purpose; the free mind doesn't need these. Looking at those trees that were so extraordinarily still on that afternoon – for you couldn't hear a machine – the road was far away and the nearby house was quiet; there was an utter silence. Even the breeze had stopped and not a single leaf stirred. The new spring grass was a delicate green; you hardly dared touch it. The earth, the trees and the pheasant that watched you were indivisible. It was all part of that extraordinary movement of life and living, the depth of which thought could never touch. The intellect may spin a lot of theories about it, build a philosophic structure around it, but the description is not the described. If you sat quietly, far away from all the past, then perhaps you would feel this; not you as a separate human being feeling it, but rather because the mind was so utterly still that there was an immense awareness without the division of the observer.

And if you wandered away a little distance there was a

farm with huge pigs – mountains of flesh, pink, snorting, ready for the market. They said it was a very good money-making business. You would often see a lorry come up a winding, rough farm road and there would be fewer pigs the next day. 'But we must live', they said, and the beauty of the earth is forgotten.

*From* BULLETIN 8, 1970

## Freedom is Order

If you are a city dweller perhaps you have never experienced the strange menace of an unfrequented wood. It was a deer sanctuary, quite close to the ugly city with its noise, dirt, squalor and overcrowded streets and houses. Very few people came to this wood. One very rarely came across anybody except a villager or two, and these were quiet people, not conscious of their own importance. Worn out by work, retiring, they were thin and rather starved, and had pain in their eyes.

This sanctuary was surrounded by high posts with barbed wire, and the deer in it were as shy as the snakes. They would see you come along and gently disappear into the bushes. There were spotted deer, full of gentle charm, with infinite curiosity, but their fear of man was stronger than their curiosity. Some of them were quite big. Then there were black ones with horns that curled straight up. They were even more shy. And beyond the fence there were others who were quite tame. They would let you come quite close. Of course you couldn't touch them, but they were not really afraid. They would stop several minutes to look at you with their ears straight up and their short tails switching. Those inside the enclosure would gather of an evening in a little meadow. You would see perhaps a

14

hundred or so. In this wood nothing was killed by man, neither the birds nor the snakes and, of course, not the deer.

One rarely saw the snakes but there were plenty of them there – the very dangerous varieties and also the harmless. One day, as we were walking on a little mound made by the ants, we saw a snake. We went up to it, quite close, perhaps a couple of feet away. It was a large, long snake, shining in the evening light, its black tongue shooting back and forth. Some labourers passing by said that it was a cobra and that we should get away from it.

The first evening that we were in this sanctuary the strange menace of the wood was felt very strongly. The sun had set, and it had become quite dark. You felt this menace enclosing you, and it went with you along the path. But the second and third day you were quite welcome there.

The sane need no discipline; only the unbalanced need the restraint, the resistance, and are tempted. The sane are aware of their desires, their urges, and temptation does not even occur to them. The healthy are strong without their knowing it. It is only the weak who know their own weakness, and so enticement and the struggle against temptation come. There really is no temptation if you keep your eyes open – not only the mental eye but also the sensory eye. The inattentive become entangled in the problems which their inattention breeds. It does not mean that the sane and the healthy have no desires. To them it is not a problem. The problem arises only when desire is made into pleasure by thought.

It is this search for pleasure against which man sets up resistance, for he is aware that there is pain involved in it, or else the environment, the culture, has bred into him the fear of continued pleasure.

Resistance in any form is violence and all our life is based on this resistance. Resistance then becomes discipline. The word 'discipline', like so many other words, is heavily loaded, interpreted according to the various families, communities, cultures. Discipline means learning. Learning does not mean a drill, an imitation, conformity. Learning about behaviour, the way of action in relationship, is the freedom to look at yourself, at your conduct.

But this seeing of yourself as you are is not possible if freedom is denied. So freedom is necessary to learn about anything, about that deer, the snake, and yourself.

Military drilling and conformity to the priest are the same, and obedience is resistance to freedom. It is strange that we haven't gone above and beyond the narrow field of suppression, control, obedience, and the authority of the book. For in all this the mind can never flourish. How can anything flourish within the darkness of fear?

But yet, order one must have; but the order of discipline, of drill, is the death of love. One must be punctual, considerate. But this consideration, if it is compelled, becomes superficial, a formal politeness. Order is not to be found in obedience. There is absolute order, as in mathematics, when the chaos of obedience is understood. It is not order first and then freedom later, but freedom *is* order.

To be desireless is to be disorderly, but to understand desire, with its pleasure, is to be orderly.

Surely, in all this, the one thing that does bring about an exquisite order – without the will, which arranges, complies, asserts – is love. And without love the established order is anarchy.

You cannot cultivate love, so you cannot possibly cultivate order. You cannot drill love into a human being. Aggression comes out of this drill, and fear.

So what is one to do? You see all this; you see the infinite mischief man is doing to man. You don't see how extraordinarily positive it is to negate; negation of the false is the truth. It is not that you replace negation with truth – but the very act of denial is the truth. The seeing is the doing, and you don't have to do anything more.

*From* BULLETIN 10, 1974

## Intelligence and Instant Action

It was very early in the morning and the valley was full of silence. The sun was not yet up behind the hills and the snow peaks were still dark. For many days now the sun had been clear, strong and rather hot. It wouldn't last, and yet this morning again the sky was very blue, the sun began to touch the snow peak, and to the west there were dark clouds. The air was clean. At that altitude the mountains seemed very near. They stood aloof, alone, and there was both that strange feeling of nearness and a sense of vast distance. As you looked at them you were aware of the age of the earth and your own impermanence. You passed away and they remained, the mountains, the hills, the green fields and the river. They would always be there, and you with your worries, your insufficiencies and sorrow would pass away.

It is always this impermanency that has made man seek something beyond the hills, investing it with permanency, with divinity, with beauty, which he in himself has not. But this doesn't answer his agonies, allay his sorrow or mischief. On the contrary it gives new life to his violence and cruelties. His gods, his utopias, his worship of the State do not end his suffering.

The magpie on the fir tree had seen the little mouse hurrying across the road, and in a second it was caught and carried off. There was only a sound of distant cowbells and of a stream rushing down the valley, but slowly the quiet morning was lost in the noise of trucks and a hammering across the road where a new house was going up.

Is there individuality at all? Or only a collective mass of varied forms of conditioning? After all, the so-called

individual is the world, the culture, the social and economic
environment. He is the world and the world is him; and all
the mischief and misery begin when he separates himself
from the world and pursues his particular talent or ambition, inclination and pleasure. We don't seem to realize
deeply that we are the world, not only at the obvious level,
but also at the core of our being. In fulfilling a particular
talent we seem to think we are expressing ourselves as individuals and, resisting every form of encroachment, insist
on its fulfilment. It is not the talent, the pleasure or the will
that make us individuals. The will, whatever little talent
one has, and the drive of pleasure are part of this whole
structure of the world.

We are not only slaves of the culture in which we have
been brought up; we are also slaves to the vast cloud of
misery and sorrow of all humanity, to the vastness of its
confusion, violence and brutality. We never seem to pay
attention to the accumulated sorrow of man. Nor are we
aware of the terrible violence which has been gathering
generation after generation. We are concerned rightly with
the outward change or reformation of the social structure
with its injustice, wars, poverty, but we try to change it
either through violence or the slow way of legislation. In
the meantime there is poverty, war, hunger and the mischief
that exists between man and man. We seem totally to
neglect paying attention to these vast accumulated clouds
which man has been gathering for centuries upon centuries
– sorrow, violence, hatred and the artificial differences of
religion and race. These are there, as the outward structure
of society is there, as real, as vital, as effective. We neglect
these hidden accumulations and concentrate on the outward
reformation. This division is perhaps the greatest cause of
our decline.

What is important is to consider life not as an inner
and outer, but as a whole, as a total undivided movement.
Then action has quite a different meaning, for then it is

not partial. It is fragmented or partial action that adds to the cloud of misery. The good is not the opposite of evil. The good has no relation to evil, and the good cannot be pursued. It flowers only when suffering is not.

How is man then to extricate himself from this confusion, violence and sorrow? Certainly not through the operation of the will with all its factors and determination, resistance and strife. The perception or the understanding of this is intelligence. It is this intelligence that puts away all the combinations of sorrow, violence and strife. It is like seeing a danger. Then there is instant action – not the action of will which is the product of thought. Thought is not intelligence. Intelligence can use thought, but when thought contrives to capture this intelligence for its own uses, then it becomes cunning, mischievous, destructive.

So intelligence is neither yours nor mine. It doesn't belong to the politician, the teacher or the saviour. This intelligence is not measurable. It is really a state of nothingness.

*From* BULLETIN II, 1971

# *The River*

AMSTERDAM, HOLLAND, MAY 1968

The river was especially wide here, deep and clean. Higher up was the very ancient city, perhaps one of the oldest in the world. But it was a mile or so away, and all the filth of the town seemed to have been cleansed by the river, and here the waters were clean, especially in mid-stream. On this side of the bank there were a lot of buildings, not particularly beautiful, but on the other side was freshly sown winter wheat, for the river rises twenty or thirty feet during the rainy season and so the soil on both banks is rich – and beyond the banks were villages, trees and fields of wheat and a kind of nourishing grain.

It was beautiful country, open, flat and spreading to the horizon. The trees especially were very old – the tamarind, the mango – and in the evening, just as the sun was setting, there would come upon the land a sense of extraordinary peace – a benediction which you never find in any church or temple.

On this side of the river bank there were four sannyasis, monks, each selling his own wares – gods. They were shouting and a crowd gathered round each of them. But the one who shouted most, repeated Sanskrit words and was covered with beads and other insignia of his profession, attracted most people, and presently you saw the other monks slip away, leaving only this one with his gods, chants and rosaries.

Imagination and romanticism deny love, for love is its own eternity. Man has sought through various gods, ideologies and hopes, something that is not bound by time. The birth of a new baby is not the indication of something eternal. Life comes and goes. There is death, there is suffering and all the mischief that man can make, and this movement of change, decay and birth is still within the cycle of time.

Time is thought; and thought is the outcome of the past. That which has continuity – the cause which produces the effect and the effect which becomes the cause in turn – is part of this movement of time. In this trap of time man has been caught and he uses every device of romance and imagination to bring about a counterfeit of what he calls eternity. And out of this comes the desire, with its pleasure, for immortality, a deathless state which he hopes to experience through the images of the mind.

Religions have offered a counterfeit of the real. The most earnest are aware of all this and of the mischief that has come through the false. There is a state which is not imagination or romantic fancy, which is not of time nor the product of thought and experience. But to come upon it, all the counterfeit coins which we have treasured must be thrown away – buried so deeply that another cannot find them. For the other thinks that he must go through those things which you have thrown away, and that is why what you throw away must never be discovered by another. For out of this comes imitation, and false coins are minted. To deny them needs no effort, no strong will nor the attraction of something greater; you put them away very simply because you see their futility, their danger and their inherent nuisance value and vulgarity.

The mind cannot manufacture the thing called eternity – as it cannot cultivate love. Nor can eternity be discovered by a mind that is seeking it. And the mind that is not seeking it is a wasted mind. The mind is a current, very deep at the centre and very shallow at the periphery – like the river that has a strong current in the middle and quiet waters at its banks.

But the deep current has the volume of memory behind it, and this memory is the continuity that passes the town, that gets sullied, that becomes clear again. The volume of memory gives the strength, the drive, the aggression and the refinement. It is this deep memory that knows itself to be ashes of the past, and it is this memory that has to come to an end.

There is no method to end it, no coin with which to buy a new state. The seeing of all this is the ending of it. It is only when this vast volume ends that there is a new beginning. The word is not the real; the measurement of the word denies the actual.

*From* BULLETIN 12, 1971–2

# What is Relationship?

The announcement said that the flight had not yet left Milan because of fog and would we all wait patiently for an hour or more; and we waited. We were all going to Rome and there was a large crowd in that waiting-room, the very smart, the long-haired ones and the short-haired; a boy had his arm around a girl, completely oblivious to all the others, and another boy with a guitar began to strum on it. Some smoked and there was considerable drinking. It was hot in the room and there was a strong smell of cheap scent.

What is relationship? What relationship have that boy and girl, or that smart woman with her husband, that older woman with her son who looked bored and was being taken abroad to be shown the ancient towns of Italy? How can there be relationship between a man and a woman, or anybody, if one is ambitious, self-absorbed in that ambition, utterly self-centred? You can see the hardness in the faces of those whose whole activities go round the 'me' and the 'you'. There may be a physical contact, and probably all relationship, the superficial or the so-called deep, remains there. How can you be related to another if you are suspicious, if you think you are always right and never admit the feeling of being wrong? That man with ancient pride of race or imagined importance, what can his relationship be except physical or superficial? How can two neurotic people, living in the same house, calling themselves husband and wife, have any kind of relationship? There are couples seemingly happy together who have grown close through trouble, sorrow and pain, with many regrets and failures – you would say that they were happy in their relationship, both physical and otherwise, but how can one have any relationship with the other if the 'me' is all-important, if one is jealous, arrogant, the other yielding? Obviously, good relationship cannot exist with any of this.

There are people who are completely absorbed in each other, who do things together with very few outside interests, satisfied to live in the same room, not going out of an evening. Such relationship is perhaps very unusual, but life isn't just good relationship. It is something much more, vastly beyond the self-satisfying movement of happy relationship. To be really related to another is possible only when ambition, suspicion, competition, the sense of possession, with all their bitterness, anger and frustrations, are totally absent.

Such relationship is rare, but without that rarity life is caught in trivialities. Life includes death, love and the understanding of pleasure, and something far beyond all these. The 'truth' of the analyst or the myth in which the religious people wallow has obviously nothing to do with reality. Without coming upon that reality, however good the relationship may be, it must remain superficial, casual, or yielding and resisting. Without that sense of the beauty of the real, relationship becomes inevitably a narrowing process.

But the people in the waiting-room, bored, annoyed at the delay, would not want any other kind of relationship than that which they had.

A well-known writer got into conversation with us, and going beyond the casual, we began to talk of serious things, of man's suffering, the incredible mythology of the church and the exploitation of man for so many centuries by an idea which he calls Truth, or God, and of the various political divisions which the writer, as a Communist, maintained were the only solution. Can suffering, we asked, can the conflict of jealousy in love, possessiveness and the demand for power and position be solved by a political dictum? 'Oh!' he said, 'I am not suffering — they are

23

suffering; this is love, this conflict, this jealousy, antagonism and fear – without these love is not.'

Just then the voice on the loudspeaker said we should board our flight. Soon we climbed to 30,000 feet, and below us was Mont Blanc and, presently, Genoa, Florence and the curving bays of the blue Mediterranean. It was a lovely day, clear, sparkling and full of light.

*From* BULLETIN 13, 1972

## The Mediocre Mind

### MALIBU, CALIFORNIA, DECEMBER 1971

It had been raining for several days, a steady downpour, and strong winds were blowing from the north-east. But this morning it was perfectly clear – blue sky, warm sun, and the sea was blue.

Sitting in the car, in a shopping district, one looks at all those shops filled with so many things and at the people rushing in and rushing out, buying all manner of goods. In the Western world it was the great holiday, and the noise, the bustle, the endless chatter of people seemed to fill the air, and in the shops everyone seemed so ravenous, so hungry to buy things.

Watching all this – the marvellous blue sky, the still sea and all these people with their greed and anxieties, one wonders where it is all going to end. And one asks why the world has become this way, so utterly bourgeois, if one can use that word. I don't know how you translate that word – what it means to you. Either you can give it a very superficial meaning and brush it aside, or examine what the implications of that word are. Why does this narrow, limited, petty mind override and seem to conquer all other minds and feelings and activities in the world? What is a bourgeois? One uses that word rather hesitatingly because it has so many political overtones, and it is used contemptuously by so many people. And in this contempt there is a feeling that they are part of it. So it would be rather interesting to find out what it means to be a bourgeois. Obviously it is a person to whom property, money and self-interest are dominant, although he may not own property, or have a lot of money, or be attached to either. There are many such people in the world. In the religious field and the world of artists and intellectuals self-interest also persists. So it may be that a bourgeois mind is this factor of self-interest. Again, that expression 'self-interest' is rather difficult to define. It has got so many subtle meanings – there are so many ways of interpreting it. But if one can look at it, go into it a little more deeply, self-interest, however wide it may be, however extended in many fields, has a narrowing quality, a narrowing activity, a limiting, restrictive action. The religious man, the monk, the sannyasi, may have renounced worldly things – property, money, position and even perhaps prestige – but his self-interest has only been transferred to a higher level. He identifies himself with his saviour, with his guru, with his belief. And this very identification, this endeavour to invest all his thoughts and feelings in a figure, in an image, in some mythical hope, constitutes self-interest. So where there is self-interest, one would think there is the very root of this terrible nationalism, this division of people, of races, of countries. Such self-interest brings about the narrowing of the mind, so that it loses elasticity and quick, perceptive action. The technician has a quick adaptability in the field of technique; he may change from one technique to another, from one business to another, or even from one belief to another, or one nationality to another, but this limited adaptability and elasticity of the mind do not offer freedom. How can a man who has invested in a particular belief or ideology have a mind and a heart that are infinitely

25

pliable, like a blade of grass that yields but still remains without breaking? So, the bourgeois is one who is attached to property, money and self-interest. You may ask your wife or your friend if there is self-interest in your relationship. If you want her or him to conform to the image that you have about them, that is self-interest. But to have no image and yet to point out certain physical, psychological facts is not self-interest.

Considering all this – the blue sky, the expanse of it, and seeing where the sea and sky meet at the horizon in that straight, marvellous line, and seeing all the hectic shopping for the holiday in which you kill trees and birds and animals, and all these people, smoking, drinking, flirting, riding in expensive or small cars – ask yourself, are you a bourgeois? You may be an artist, a politician, a businessman, or any ordinary man going about his little job, or the woman in the kitchen or in the office – whatever you are, if there is any kind of self-interest in your relationship with another, in the position you hold, or in some belief or ideology – then, inevitably, you have a narrow, petty little mind. You may be doing good work, you may be generous in your help to others or be so-called happily married; you may talk of love, you may love your wife, your children or your friends, but if there is any of this destructive self-interest, there is the stamp of mediocrity that gives such great importance to property, position, money and power. This petty little mind cannot go beyond the wall, the barriers that man has built around himself.

And so, sitting in the car, waiting for somebody, the warm sun on your face and on the faces of those who pass by, you look at all those people and you wonder what has happened to humanity. The young fall into a groove as much as the old. Fashions change, and so the grooves change also. But being caught in any tradition, in any condition, doesn't give to the mind this strange quality of elasticity. Again, that word needs explaining. The mind, or consciousness, can stretch with great knowledge, with experience, with suffering, or with great joy. Pleasure doesn't help the elasticity of the mind – joy does. But the pursuit of joy, or the pursuit of enjoyment, which becomes pleasure, forbids any kind of freedom, quickness, elasticity. As we said, the mind can move from technique to technique, from job to job, from action to action, from belief to a new ideology, but this isn't really elasticity. As long as the mind is tethered or bound to any point, to any experience, to any knowledge, it cannot go very far. And as the content of consciousness makes up consciousness, the very content prevents the freedom, the quickness, the marvellous sense of movement. The content of consciousness becomes self-interest. The content may be that you give importance to a piece of furniture, or to some technique, or to some belief or experience: that experience, that knowledge, that incident becomes the centre of self-interest. The emptying of consciousness of all its content is to have total movement in perception and action.

*From* BULLETIN 14, 1972

## *To be Alone*

Meditation is the act of being alone. The act is entirely different from the activities of isolation. The very nature of the 'me', the self, the ego, is to isolate itself, through concentration, through various forms or methods of meditation, and through the daily activities of separation. But to be alone is not a withdrawal from the world. The world of man is gregarious; it is the interrelationship of influence, of opinion, and the weight of tradition. It is the entertainment of thought and the activity of self-absorption. This in-inevitably leads to loneliness and self-isolating misery.

To be alone is only possible when the mind is outside the influence of society; when inwardly there is freedom from the social disorder. This freedom is virtue, and virtue is always alone; the morality of society is the continuance of disorder. Meditation is transcending this disorder and is not the private pleasure of visions and expanding experiences. These experiences are ever isolating.

Love is not separative, and as love cannot be cultivated so aloneness is not a thing of thought. It comes as naturally as the sunrise when there is freedom from the activities of thought.

The evening sun was on the new grass and there was splendour in every blade. The spring leaves were just overhead, so delicate that when you touched them you did not feel them, so vulnerable that a passing child could tear them. And the blue sky was over the trees and the blackbirds were singing. The water of the canal was so still that you could literally not distinguish the reflection from the real. There was a duck's nest with half a dozen or more eggs in it, which she had very carefully covered up with dry leaves. When you came back you saw her sitting on them, pretending not to be there. And as you walked further along that canal, amidst the tall beeches with those marvellous new leaves, there was another duck with twelve or more chicks all around her, probably just hatched that very morning. Some of them would be eaten during the night by the rats, and when you came back the next day there were a few missing. The duck on her nest was still there. It was a beautiful evening, full of that strange glory which is the heart of spring. You stood there without a thought, feeling every tree and every blade of grass, and hearing that bus, loaded with people, passing by.

After all, it is becoming more and more difficult even to be physically alone. Most people don't want to be alone; they are afraid to be alone; they are occupied, and they want to be occupied, from the moment they wake up until the moment they go to bed, and even then they are haunted by dreams. And those who live alone, in the caves or as the monks in their cells, are never alone, for they live with their images, their thoughts, and the practices which promise them future fulfilment. They are never alone; they are full of knowledge and full of the darkness of the cave or the cell.

One must really be an outsider, not belonging to anything or to anybody. But you cannot fight your way out, for then you still belong to it. The very action of fighting your way out is the action which makes society tick. And so there is neither outside nor inside. As soon as you are aware that you are outside, you are in. So you must die to society, so that the new life comes into being without your knowing it. The new is not an experience; to know the new is to be the old. And so walk in solitude, though you live in society.

*From* BULLETIN 21, 1974

## The Pitcher Can Never be Filled

Meditation is like going to a well, the waters of which are inexhaustible, with a pitcher that is always empty. The pitcher can never be filled. What is important is the drinking of the waters and not how full the pitcher is. The pitcher must be broken to drink the water. The pitcher is the centre which is always seeking – and so it can never find.

To seek is to deny the truth that is right in front of you. Your eyes must see that which is the nearest; and the seeing of that is a movement without end. He who seeks projects that which he seeks and so he lives in an illusion, always striving within the limits of his own shadow. Not to seek is to find; and the finding is not in the future – it is there, where you do not look. The looking is ever present, from which all life and action takes place. Meditation is the blessing of this action.

Seeking is a personal drive from the centre – to attain, to belong, to hold. In inquiry there is freedom from the very beginning; looking is the freedom from the weight of yesterday.

*From* BULLETIN 22, 1974

## The Nature of Humility

The essence of austerity is humility. To know humility is to deny it. You can know only vanity. You can be conscious of vanity but you cannot be conscious of humility. Austerity, the austerity of the monk or of the saint, is the harsh movement of becoming, which is illusion. This harshness is of violence, imitation, obedience, in which there is no anonymity. The monk and the saint may take a different name but this name is the cloak that covers the wounds of conflict. And this is the same for every one of us, for we are all idealists. We know vanity, and cannot know humility. Our humility is the opposite of vanity, and all opposites contain each other. The 'becoming', however secret, however anonymous, can never be of the nature of humility. Humility has no opposite, and only those that have opposites can know each other.

Denying pride is not knowing humility. The dying to the known is the positive of the unknown. You can die to the known consciously, deliberately, with the full knowledge of all its implications, but there is no knowing of that which is not known. You cannot know the unknown, as humility. In the field of becoming the movement is from the known to the known; when we die to this, something else comes into being which cannot be comprehended by a mind that is still within the limitations of the known, the memory, the experience, the knowledge. The 'being' is not the end of 'becoming'. When it is recognized as 'being' it is still part of the 'becoming', in which effort, struggle, confusion and misery are involved.

Meditation is not a trick of the mind confronting itself with an insoluble problem and so forcing itself to be quiet. A stunned mind obviously has become insensitive, not responsive, and so incapable of seeing anything new. And the new is not the opposite of the old.

Meditation is the uncovering of this whole process of becoming and being – the negation of becoming in order to be. All this can be seen by a meditative mind at a glance, and this glance doesn't involve time at all. Seeing truth is not a matter of time; either you see or you don't see. The incapacity to see cannot become capable of seeing.

So negation is the movement of meditation, and there is no way, no path, no system that can lead a chattering, shallow mind to the heights of bliss. The seeing of this instantly is the truth that frees the shallow mind from itself.

And humility is always at the beginning – but there is no beginning and no end. And this is the bliss beyond measure.

*From* BULLETIN 24, 1974–5

## Meditation and Love

The whole point of meditation is not to follow the path laid down by thought to what it considers to be truth, enlightenment or reality. There is no path to truth. The following of any path leads to what thought has already formulated

31

and, however pleasant or satisfying, it is not truth. It is a fallacy to think that a system of meditation, the constant practising of that system in daily life for a few given moments, or the repetition of it during the day, will bring about clarity or understanding. Meditation lies beyond all this and, like love, cannot be cultivated by thought. As long as the thinker exists to meditate, meditation is merely a part of that self-isolation which is the common movement of one's everyday life.

Love is meditation. Love is not a remembrance, an image sustained by thought as pleasure, nor the romantic image which sensuality builds; it is something that lies beyond all the senses and beyond the economic and social pressures of life. The immediate realization of this love, which has no root in yesterday, is meditation; for love is truth, and meditation is the discovery of the beauty of this truth. Thought cannot discover this; it can never say: 'I have discovered' or 'I have captured that love which is of heaven.'

*From* BULLETIN 29, 1976

## Meditation and Experience

Is there a new experience in meditation? The desire for experience, the higher experience which is beyond and above the daily or the commonplace, is what keeps the well-spring empty. The craving for more experience, for visions, for higher perception, for some realization or other, makes the mind look outward, which is no different from its dependence on environment and people. The curious part of meditation is that an event is not made into an experience. It is there, like a new star in the heavens, without memory taking it over and holding it, without the habitual process of recognition and response in terms of like and dislike. Our search is always outgoing; the mind seeking any experience is outgoing. Inward-going is not a search at all; it is perceiving. Response is always repetitive, for it comes always from the same bank of memory.

*From* BULLETIN 31, 1977

## To a Young Man

He was a young man, recently married, and he said he hadn't too good a job, but it gave him and his wife enough money to live on. He had been educated in one of the universities, had a somewhat sharp mind, and belonged to one of those ancient communities to whom a religious life was much more significant than the way of the world.

'My education,' he continued, 'has made my mind rather dull. It has cultivated my memory and probably nothing else. I have taken several degrees but all that has left me somewhat empty and arid. I seem to be losing all feeling, all concern, and falling into a routine; and I can see my sexual activities also becoming part of the same pattern. I don't know what to do. After hearing you the other day I thought perhaps that by talking things over with you I might free myself from the dead weight of my job and of my daily habits. As I am quite young I could change my job, but I know that however interesting it may be it will soon become a routine. My wife and I have talked this over. She couldn't come this morning, so I am talking for her as well as for myself.' He had a nice smile, and society had not quite destroyed him yet.

Routine and habit are our everyday life. Some are aware of their habits, others are not. If one becomes aware of habits – the repetitious movement of the hand or of the mind – one can put an end to them with comparative ease. But what is important in all this is to understand, not intellectually, the mechanism of habit-forming which gradually destroys or blunts all feeling. This machinery is the enormous lethargy which is part of our heritage, as tradition is. We don't want to be disturbed, and it is this lethargy which builds routine. Once having learnt, we function according to what we already know, adding to or modifying what we already know.

The fear of change strengthens habit, not only physically but also in the very brain cells themselves. So having once become established in a routine, we keep going, like a tramcar along its rails. We take things for granted in all relationships, and this is one of the major factors of insensitivity. So habit becomes a natural thing. Then we say: why should one pay attention to these things that one does every day? And so inattention cultivates habit; and then we are caught. Then the problem begins of how to be free of habit. And then there is conflict. And thus conflict becomes the way of life we accept naturally!

So when one sees all this – all the ways of habit, which is to function according to established memory, to operate from that memory – when there is an awareness of this, then one comes upon the way of pleasure. Because, after all, what we deeply want is pleasure and all our values are based on it. Pleasure is the constant factor for which we are willing to sacrifice, which we defend, for which we are willing to be violent and so on. But, if we watch pleasure, we will soon see that it, too, becomes a habit, and when that habit of pleasure is denied there is discomfort, pain and sorrow. And to avoid this we fall into another trap of pleasure. One can get used to beauty or to ugliness – to the beauty of a tree or to the squalor of the road. We hang up a picture in the room and we look at it, and soon it has become a habit. Or, as some people do, we change the picture hoping thereby to keep the vision sharp. This is merely another trick to overcome insensitivity.

So this is the way of life we have accepted. It is what is happening to us from morning to night, and throughout the night. So the whole of consciousness is mechanical in the sense that it is a constant movement, activity, within the borders of pleasure and pain. To go beyond these borders man has tried many different ways. But everything is soon reduced to the monotony of habit and pleasure; and if you have the energy you become very active, outwardly. Now the whole point of this is to see – actually, non-verbally – what is really taking place. To see non-verbally means to see without the observer, for the observer is the essence of habit and contradiction, which is memory. So seeing is never habitual because the seeing is non-accumulative. When you see from the accumulation you see through habits. So, seeing is action without habit.

After all, love is not habit – whereas pleasure is. So the act of seeing is the only natural thing; seeing the natural inheritance of the animal in us, which is violent, aggressive and competitive. If you could understand this one thing, which is really of primary importance – the act of seeing – then there is no accumulation as the 'me' and the 'mine', then there is no habit-forming at all, with the routine and the boredom of it all. So to see what is, is to love.

*From* BULLETIN 36, 1979

## *Love is not Thought*

GSTAAD, SWITZERLAND, 3 AUGUST 1981

The valley runs from east to west; the east end tapers off to a narrow canyon with a 6,000-feet mountain over which the morning sun comes, casting long deep shadows and endless silence. There is an old oak tree – several hundred years old – which catches the morning sun, golden and motionless. The very highest leaf is breathless in its stillness. The mourning dove begins its peculiar long, soft cooing, answered by its mate. And the day has begun. The great-horned owl had stopped its hooting as the early spring dawn was showing the outlines of the rocky mountain and the long lines of wooded hills. Before the sun came up, great silences seemed to cover the land. And how beautiful was the earth, timeless in its vastness. It is our earth, ours and not of any group, community or nation. It is ours; it belongs to every one of us.

The road is well-engineered, smooth, wide, without too many sharp turns as it climbs, passing miles upon miles of well-kept orange orchards and endless avocado groves, which go down the gullies and up the whole hillside, all to be watered and cared for. The valley is filled with the scent of orange blossoms and avocados. The road passes through the highest point, perhaps 5,000 feet, then it descends slowly into the desert. At the highest point of the road the car stopped. To the south the high, vast hills were covered with trees and bushes, purple and yellow flowers; to the north there was no tree; it was barren, rocky, vast, stretching to the horizon, utterly unspoiled, every rock as it must have been for a thousand years. Immense space and immeasurable silence.

Solitude is one thing and being alone is another. Solitude can be isolation, an escape, an unwanted thing; but to be alone without the burden of life, with that utter freedom in which time/thought has never been, is to be with the universe. In solitude there is despairing loneliness, a sense of being abandoned, lost, craving for some kind of relationship, like a ship lost at sea. All our daily activity leads to this isolation, with its endless conflicts and miseries, and rare joys thrown in. This isolation is corruption, manifested in politics, in business and of course in organized religions. Corruption exists in the very high places and on the very doorstep. To be tied is corruption; any form of attachment leads to it, whether it be to a belief, faith, ideal, experience, or any conclusion. Psychological corruption is the common factor in the human. Money, status, power are the superficial responses of the inward corruption of the mounting pleasure of desire, the image that thought builds around the movement of desire. Corruption is fragmentation.

In that vast space between the blue, clear sky and the beauty of the earth, consciousness had come to an end. All the senses were fully awake to the unpolluted air, the smell of the desert and distant flowers, the movement of the lizard on the warm rock and the utter silence. It was not only the silence of high altitude, that strange silence just after the sun has set, or that which seems to descend on the earth with the beginning of dawn, away from all cities and noisy villages, but also that profound silence which the noise of thought has never touched. It is that silence that has no measure, of such purity and clarity that it goes far beyond all the movement of consciousness. Time had literally stopped.

That silence accompanied us as the car ran down through the orchards and the groves. There civilization began, the incredible vulgarity, the brutal haste and the immodesty of humans, everyone asserting his presence, and the rich showing their power and will. Even that excellent motor seemed to have become suddenly silent, which of course is nonsense. The morning papers in their editorials were stating what the effect would be if and when a nuclear bomb exploded over a great city: several millions vaporized, society in ruins and primordial chaos. And so on, horror upon horror. And humanity puts its faith in politicians and governments.

Any specialist – the surgeon, the archbishop, the chef or the plumber – uses only a part of the brain, narrowing down its total activity. The politician and the guru employ only a small part of the extraordinary capacity and energy of the brain. This limited, partial activity is creating havoc in the world. This small part of the brain is functioning in all religions when they repeat their rituals, their meaningless words, their gestures of 2,000 or 5,000 years of tradition, according to how they have been programmed. Some do it gracefully in fine garments, and others crudely. It is the same in government circles, the corruption of power. The little part may accumulate great knowledge, but that very knowledge only further strengthens a part of the brain. The ascension of man can never be through knowledge, for it is never complete; it is ever within the shadow of ignorance. The ultra-intelligent machine, the fast-developing computer, which is programmed by experts, will overtake and outrun man's thought and its slow capacities; it will learn faster, correcting its own mistakes, solving its own problems. The human being has not resolved any of his psychological problems, the issues that have become so complex. It appears that he has been burdened with them from the most ancient of days. We are still carrying on with these problems, of government, religion, relationship, violence, wars and the pollution of the earth. They will remain insoluble as long as only a part of the brain is functioning, as long as one is programmed to be American, British, French and so on, as long as one is a Catholic, Hindu, Muslim. One is, it appears, so utterly unaware of how conditioned, programmed, that little part of the brain is. This gives this programming an illusory sense of security, a verbal structure against the barbarians. But man is the only barbarian; he himself is the cause of all the corruption and horror that is taking place in the world. He is totally and completely responsible for all that is happening around him.

This little part of the brain is our consciousness; it is the seat of time, measure, space and thought. Time is evolution both biologically and psychologically; it is the sun rising and setting; it is the sense of becoming. Measure is what is

and what should be, the ideal to be achieved, the violent
becoming peaceful, achieving the constant, the continuous
becoming; comparison, imitation, conformity; the better
and the more. Space is the vast expanse of the earth, the
heavens and the little space in crowded cities, and space, if
any, in consciousness. Thought is the master. Thought is
the most dominant factor in human life. There is no Eastern
thought or Western thought; there is only thought which
may be expressed in many different ways, but it is still the
movement of thought. Thought is common to all mankind,
from the most primitive to the most highly educated.
Thought has put men on the moon; thought has built the
atom bomb; it has built all the temples, the great cathedrals
with all the things in them called sacred, the elaborate
rituals, the dogmas, the beliefs, faith and so on. It has built
the computer and the programme that goes into it. It has
helped mankind in countless different ways, but it has also
bred wars and all the instruments of death. It has projected
ideals, enormous violence, tortures, divided humanity into
nations, classes and innumerable religions which have
divided man against himself and set man against man.
Love is not thought with its remembrances and images.

Thought sustains and nourishes consciousness. The content of consciousness is the never-ending movement of
thought, the desires, the conflicts, the fears, the pursuit of
pleasures, pain, loneliness, sorrow. Love, compassion with
its incorruptible intelligence, is beyond this limited consciousness. It may not be divided into higher or lower, for
the high or the low is still consciousness, ever noisy, ever
chattering. Consciousness is all time, all measure, all space,
for it is born of thought. Thought can never in any circumstances be whole; it may speculate about that which is
whole and indulge in the verbalization and the experience
of it, but thought can never perceive its beauty, its immensity.

For thought is the barren child of experience and

knowledge, which can never be complete, whole. So thought will always be limited, fragmented. The problems thought has brought to man thought tries vainly to resolve and thus increasingly perpetuates them. Only when it realizes its utter incapacity psychologically to resolve the problems and conflicts it has brought about, can perception, insight, end them.

*From* BULLETIN 56, 1989

## What Does Relationship Mean?

### SAANEN, SWITZERLAND, AUGUST 1981

The love of trees is, or should be, a part of our nature, like breathing. They are part of the earth like us, full of beauty with that strange aloofness. They are so still, full of leaves, rich and full of light, casting long shadows and wild with joy when there is a storm. Every leaf, even at the very top, is dancing in the slight breeze, and the shadows are welcoming in the strong sun. As you sit with your back against the trunk, if you are very quiet, you establish a lasting relationship with nature. Most people have lost that relationship; they look at all those mountains, valleys, the streams and the thousand trees as they pass by in their cars or walk up the hills chattering, but they are too absorbed in their own problems to look and be quiet. The smoke is going up in a single column across the valley, and below a lorry goes by, heavy with logs of recently cut trees, their bark still on them. A group of boys and girls passes by chattering and shattering the stillness of the wood.

The death of a tree is beautiful in its ending, unlike man's. A dead tree in a desert, stripped of its bark, polished by the sun and the wind, all its naked branches open to the heavens, is a wondrous sight. A great redwood, many, many hundreds of years old, is cut down in a few minutes to make fences, seats, and build houses or enrich the soil in a garden. That marvellous giant is gone. Man is pushing deeper and deeper into the forests, destroying them for pasture and houses. The wilds are disappearing. There is a valley, whose surrounding hills are perhaps the oldest on earth, where cheetahs, bears and the deer one once saw have entirely disappeared, for man is everywhere. The beauty of the earth is slowly being destroyed and polluted. Cars and tall buildings are appearing in the most unexpected places. When you lose your relationship with nature and the vast heavens, you lose your relationship with man.

He came with his wife and did most of the talking. She was rather shy, intelligent-looking. He was rather overbearing and appeared to be aggressive. He said they had been to some of the talks after reading one or two books and had heard some of the dialogues.

'We have really come to talk over with you personally our major problem, which I hope you won't mind. We have two children, a boy and a girl; they are at school, fortunately for them. We don't want to inflict on them the tensions between us, though they will feel them sooner or later. We two are very fond of each other; I won't use the word "love", as I have understood what you mean by that word. We were married fairly young; we have a nice house with a smallish garden. Money is not our problem. She has money of her own and I work, though my father left me some. We haven't come to you as a marriage counsellor, but we want to discuss with you, if you don't mind, our relationship. My wife is rather reserved, but I am sure she will join in the discussion presently. We had agreed that I should lead off. We are greatly troubled about our relationship. We have talked about it quite often, but nothing has come out of it. After this introduction, the question I would like to put is: what is wrong with our relationship, or what is right relationship?'

What is your relationship with those clouds, full of evening light, or with those silent trees? It is not an irrelevant question. Do you see those children playing in that field, the old car? When you see all those, what is your reaction, if one may ask?

'I am not sure what it is. I like to see children playing. So does my wife. I have no special feelings about those clouds or that tree. I have not thought about them; probably I have never even looked at them.'

His wife said, 'I have. They mean something to me, but I can't put it into words. The children out there could be my children. After all I am a mother.'

Do look, sir, at those clouds and the tree as though you were looking for the first time. Look at them without thought interfering or wandering off. Look at them without naming them as a cloud or a tree. Just look with your heart and eyes. They are of the earth as we are, as those children are, even that old car. The very naming is part of thought.

'To look at those without verbalizing them seems almost impossible. The very form is the word.'

So words play a very important part in our lives. Our life, it appears, is a network of complicated, interrelated words. Words have a great impact upon us, like 'god', 'democracy', 'freedom', 'totalitarianism'. These words conjure up familiar images. The words 'wife' and 'husband' are part of our everyday currency. But the word 'wife' is not actually the living person, with all her complexities and troubles. So the word is never the actual. When the word becomes all-important, the living, the actual is neglected.

'But I can't escape from the word and the image that the word brings up.'

One cannot separate the word and the image. The word is the image. To observe without word/image is the problem.

'That's impossible, sir.'

If one may point out, you haven't attempted seriously to

do this. The word 'impossible' blocks your doing it. Don't, please, say it is possible or impossible, but simply do it. Let us go back to your question: what is right relationship? You will, one is sure, find out for yourself what is right when we understand relationship. What does relationship mean to you?

'Let me think. It means so many things depending on circumstances. One day it is a particular response, and on another it has a wholly different significance. It's responsibility, boredom, irritation, sensual responses and the urge to escape from it all.'

This is what you call relationship. It is different degrees of sensory responses, of sentiment – romantic, if one is inclined that way – tenderness, attachment, loneliness, fear and so on (apprehension more than actual fear). This is called relationship with one particular person or another. You are also related to your ideals, hopes, to your experiences, conclusions. All this is you and your relationship with another; and the other person is similar to you, though she may be biologically, culturally, outwardly different. So does it not indicate that you are ever active within egocentricity and she is active in a similar manner? Two parallel lines never meeting?

'I am beginning to see what you mean, but do please continue.'

It becomes clear that there is no actual relationship. One is basically concerned about oneself, one's own pleasure, yielding to another in satisfaction and so on and on. Let's put it differently. Why are human beings so self-centred, consciously, or in the deepest recesses of their being selfish? Why? The non-domesticated animals appear not to be egocentric as humans are. If we are to discover for ourselves what is right relationship, we must go into this question very deeply. Perception without motive is to experiment. Most of us find it difficult to observe without some kind of motive or other. Can we examine together, very objectively, what actually takes place in a relationship of two people, whether it is intimate or not? Almost all reactions are recorded in the brain, especially those that are painful or pleasurable, consciously or at a deeper level. This recording goes on from childhood until death. This recording slowly builds up an image or picture which each person has of himself. If one is married or lives with another, for a month or for years, each one has formed an image about the other – the hurts, the irritations, the harsh words, the flatteries and so on, the sensual responses, the intellectual observations, the companionship and tenderness, the imagination of fulfilment and cultural associations. These form the varying images that are awakened in different circumstances. Apart from actual physical relations, these images distort or deny a profound relationship of love, compassion with its intelligence.

'Then how or in what manner can these images not be formed?'

Are you not putting a wrong question, sir? Who is it that prevents? Is it not another image or idea that is putting the question? Are you not still working with images, from one to the other? Such inquiries lead nowhere. When one is hurt or wounded psychologically, which one is, from childhood, the consequences of that hurt are obvious: fear of further hurts, withdrawal by building a wall around oneself, further isolation and so on – a process of neuroticism. If and when one is aware of, observes these wounds, the conflicts, then one instinctively demands how one can prevent being hurt. The ultimate image is the 'I', the self with the capital 'S' and the small 's'. When one grasps the full significance of why the brain, thought, forms these images, the truth of why these images exist, that very perception dispels all the formation of images. This is the ultimate freedom.

'What is the reason why the brain, or thought, as you say, forms images?'

Is it for security? To be safe from all danger? To be certain, to avoid confusion? Whatever small part of the brain is functioning, to function well, efficiently, it must feel certain, safe. Whether that certainty, security, is an illusion or some invention of thought, such as faith or belief, is actually of no importance as long as that limited part of the brain feels safe, assured, certain. In this illusion we live. With the image, such as nationalism and the images in all the temples of the world, man lives and carries on with conflict, pleasure, sorrow. The forming of these images has no end. But when you perceive that they prevent, cast a shadow on, our actual and profound relationship between each other, between ourselves and that cloud, that tree and those children, then only can there be love.

*From* BULLETIN 56, 1989

## Beauty is Dangerous

SAANEN, SWITZERLAND, 11 AUGUST 1981

Beauty is dangerous. Standing on that hill one saw 300 miles of the Himalayas, almost from horizon to horizon, with deep, dark valleys, peak after peak with everlasting snow, not a house in sight, not a village, not a hut. The sun was touching the highest peaks, and all of a sudden the whole continuous range was afire. It was as though they were afire from within, a glow of incredible intensity. The valleys became darker and the silence was absolute. The earth was breathless in its splendour. As the sun rose from out of the far east, the immensity, the utter purity of those majestic mountains seemed so close one could almost touch them, but they were many hundreds of miles away.

And the day began. No wonder man has worshipped

45

them; they are sacred, to be adored from afar. All the ancients made gods of them, for there the heavenly ones made their abode. Now they are being made into ski-runs with hotels, swimming-pools and noise. But not among those implacable and incorruptible snows. Beauty is imperishable and infinitely dangerous.

Leaving that impenetrable silence, going down the rocky trail, following a stream down, passing through many varieties of pine, large deodars, the path became wide, covered with grass. It was a lovely morning, soft with the scent of a rich forest. The path took many turns and it was becoming warm. In the trees close by there was a whole group of monkeys, their faces shining in that morning sun, with long tails and grey, hairy bodies. The babies were clinging to their mothers and the whole group was quietly watching, unafraid, the solitary figure. They watched unmoving. And presently a group of sannyasis, chanting, was going down to a distant village. Their Sanskrit was precise and clear, indicating they were from the far south. Their hymn was to the morning sun, who gave life to all things and whose benediction was and is on all living things. There were about eight of them, three or four quite young, all with shaven heads, clad in saffron robes, controlled, with downcast eyes, not seeing the great trees, the thousand flowers and the green, soft hills; for beauty is dangerous – desire may be aroused.

The village was preparing its morning meal and the smell of wood fires was in the air. The children, freshly washed, were preparing for school with shouts and laughter. Amid the usual noise of the village there was a sense of sad weariness. It had its priest, the believer and the unbeliever.

It is odd how the priests, from time beyond memory, have conditioned the human brain to have faith, to believe, to obey. They were the scholars, the teachers, the law. By their conduct, noble and responsible, they were the social guardians, upholders of tradition. Through fear they controlled the kings and the people. At one time they were outside, apart from society so that they could guide it, morally, aesthetically, religiously. They gradually became the interpreters between God and man. They had power, status and the vast wealth of the temples, churches, mosques. In the East they covered their bodies in simple, distinctly coloured cloth. In the West their ritual garments became more and more symbolic, more and more expensive. Then there were those simple monks in monasteries and those in palaces. The religious heads, with their bureaucracy, held the people in faith, dogma, rituals and meaningless words. Superstition, guile, hypocrisy became the coin of all organized religions in the East and the West. And that which is most sacred went out of the window, however beautiful the window was.

So man has to begin again to discover that which is eternally sacred, never to be caught by the interpreter, the priest, the guru, by the pedlars of meditation. You have to be a light to yourself. That light can *never* be given by another, by any philosopher or psychologist, however respected by tradition.

Freedom is to stand alone, unattached and unafraid, free in the understanding of desire which breeds illusion. There is a vast strength in being alone. It is the conditioned, programmed brain that is never alone, for it is filled with knowledge. That which is programmed, religiously or technologically, is always limited. This limitation is the major factor of conflict.

Beauty is dangerous for a man of desire.

*From* BULLETIN 57, 1989

# PART II

# Questions and Answers

# Meditation and the Timeless Moment

EXCERPT FROM A DISCUSSION HELD IN NEW DELHI, 1956

*Questioner: What is involved in meditation?*

KRISHNAMURTI: The primary thing is to empty the mind completely of everything it has known; the second, a non-directed, non-controlled energy. Then, it also requires the highest form of order, order in the sense of a complete ending of the disorder brought about by contradiction, and a quality of mind that has no character. We must completely set aside the idea or practice of a method. The central issue is whether the mind – it includes the heart, the brain and the whole physical organism – can live without any distortion, without any compulsion and therefore without any effort. Please put the question to yourself; all this is meditation.

Our minds are distorted; they have been shaped by the culture in which we live, by the religious, economic structures, by the food we eat and so on. The mind is given a definite form, it is conditioned and this conditioning is a distortion. A mind can see very clearly, purely, completely, innocently, only when there is no distortion. The first move is the capacity to look – the art of listening – to look without distortion, which means the mind must be absolutely still, without a movement. Can the mind that is in constant movement be completely and absolutely quiet, without any movement, without any method, system, practice, control?

The mind must empty itself of all the past to become highly sensitive; and it cannot be sensitive if there is the burden of the past. It is only the mind that has understood all this that can put the question. And when it puts the question it has no answer, because there is no answer. The mind has become highly sensitive and therefore supremely intelligent and intelligence has no answer. It is in itself the answer. The observer has no place because intelligence is supreme.

Then the mind is no longer seeking, no longer wanting higher experiences and therefore it is not capable of control. See the beauty of it, sir. It does not control, because it is intelligent. It is operating, it is working. Therefore, in the very act of intelligence, the dual state disappears. All this is meditation. It is like a cloud that begins on a hilltop with a few little clouds, and, as it moves, it covers the whole sky, the valley, the mountains, the rivers, the human beings, the earth; it covers everything. That is meditation because meditation is the concern of all the living, not just one part of it.

Then only can the mind be absolutely still without any movement – not for the duration of that moment, because that moment has no duration, because it is not of time. Time exists only when there is the observer who experiences that silence and says: 'I wish I could have more of it.' So that moment of absolute stillness, immobility, because it is not of time, has no future or past. Therefore, that absolute motionless immobility is beyond all thought. And that moment, because it is timeless, is endless.

A mind that is free of any distortion is really the true religious mind, not a mind that goes to the temple, not a mind that reads the sacred books, not a mind that repeats rituals, however beautiful they may be, not a mind that is filled with images, imposed upon it or self-created.

Living is not separate from learning, and in this there is great beauty. For, after all, love is that. Love is compassion, passion, passion for everything. When there is love, there is no observer, there is no duality: the 'you' who love 'me' and the 'I' who love 'you'. There is only love, though it may be loving one or the thousand; there is only love.

When there is love, then you can do no wrong, do what

you will. But without love we are trying to do everything – going to the moon, the marvellous scientific discoveries – and therefore everything goes wrong. Love can only come when there is no observer. That means, when the mind is not divided in itself as the one observing and the observed, only then there is that quality of love. When you have that, that is the Supreme.

*From* BULLETIN 35, 1978

## *Fear and Confusion*

### EXTRACT FROM A DISCUSSION WITH YOUNG PEOPLE IN PARIS, APRIL 1967

KRISHNAMURTI: Confusion may be one of the principal causes of fear. Being confused and not finding a way out, we are afraid. Being in sorrow and incapable of ending sorrow, we say, despairingly, 'It is hopeless, it is this, it is that.' Now, is there a way out? Let us go into it.

When we say, 'I am confused,' do we see it as a fact? You understand what I mean? Do I realize I am hungry or is it that I'm told I am hungry? The two are entirely different. Now which is it? Do I realize I am confused or do I sense my confusion only in relation *to* something?

*Questioner: In relation to some state we imagine.*

KRISHNAMURTI: That's it. So is confusion a direct experience or only an experience to be achieved in comparison to some state which is not? Please, sirs, it is very important to discuss this. I am confused: do I realize it as I realize I am hungry, or do I realize it only in comparison to something which I have thought or achieved, or which I have understood as clarity? Sir, when you are hungry do you compare it with when you are not hungry? You don't; you are

53

hungry. In the same way, do I realize I am confused? If you realize it, then it becomes vital, then you have to find an answer.

*Questioner: Then why don't we realize it?*

KRISHNAMURTI: Wait, wait. First see the difference. When you realize that you are hungry, you act – beg, borrow or steal – you *do* something. But if you say, 'Well, I may be hungry,' then you take time, talk about it, discuss what kind of food you are going to have and so on. When you realize, your action is immediate. And that is the whole point. I am confused and I realize that any movement I make – any movement in thought or any activity initiated by thought – is still confusion. Right? Do I realize that *fact*? Which means that it is thought that is creating the confusion, and therefore the fear.

*Questioner: But the problem is that as soon as one hears that, one imagines a thoughtless state.*

KRISHNAMURTI: No, sir. You see you do not move from fact to fact; you are already far away from the fact. I am confused and I realize that whatever movement I make is still the product of confusion. When I know that, I stop; I don't invent, theorize or despair. I say, 'By Jove, I'm confused.' Then what takes place – empirically, not as a theory? What takes place when I realize I am confused and that whatever I do or think, whatever activity I hope to achieve, whatever movement I make, is the product of confusion and therefore adding more confusion – when I realize that psychologically I am confused and that psychologically any movement the psyche makes is still within the field of confusion, I stop, don't I? The movement of the psyche stops – and therefore I am not afraid *because fear is part of the confusion.*

Now is this the case with each one of us? – otherwise we cannot discuss this matter.

*Questioner: Not for me. I'm still in a despairing state.*

KRISHNAMURTI: I realize there is no way out, that the road doesn't lead anywhere, that there is an impasse. What do I do? You don't say, 'Well, I don't know what to do.' You don't stay there; you turn your back, don't you?

*Questioner: But how to realize?*

KRISHNAMURTI: That is the question: how to realize the total confusion of man, *not how to get out of it*. Then you begin to find out the causes of this confusion – because you have stopped, not because you are seeking. I don't know if you see the difference. Before, I was looking for the causes of confusion in order to clear them up; therefore my looking, my examination, was entirely different from now when, because I realize I am confused, I can see that there is no activity possible. This looking is an entirely different observation.

*Questioner: One is without a motive.*

KRISHNAMURTI: That's it. One is without motive, the other is with motive.

*Questioner: Out of confusion you see it differently because you have a motive behind it – you see what you want to, not what really is. But if you have no motive, you can see directly what is.*

KRISHNAMURTI: That's right. Please see his point, look what he has said. He says that if you have a motive, then that motive distorts, and that when you have no motive you see clearly.

*Questioner: But how can we stop having motives?*

KRISHNAMURTI: Wait, wait. You cannot stop anything, but just observe. Sir, you are missing the whole point, you are too intellectual. This is a direct problem, not an intellectual problem.

*Any* movement on my part is confusion, and that's the difficulty. Now I have realized that as long as I look with a motive, all looking is distorted. So is it possible to look without motive? It is the motive that is going to breed fear, obviously. So, a much more fundamental question is included in this: is it possible for any action to take place without motive?

*From* BULLETIN 22, 1974

## The State of not Knowing

AN EXTRACT FROM A DISCUSSION WITH STUDENTS AT
HUIZEN, HOLLAND, JUNE 1967

*Questioner: Is it not a fact that with intense awareness while you are awake, you can have the experience of watching anger come and go within yourself without it touching your consciousness?*

KRISHNAMURTI: Oh, sir! Let us be a little careful about this. Is the conscious self different from the anger? I am jealous, let us say. Is the 'I' different from the jealousy? Is that jealousy different from the person who is watching the jealousy? I am the experiencer and the thing I experience is jealousy. Is the experiencer different from the experience?

It is quite interesting to discuss this from the point of view of what is learning. I am jealous of you, I am envious of you, and I want to learn all about it, because when I learn the whole content of it, it is finished; it no longer has the bite. Now, *how* do I learn? What is learning? Apart from learning a language – how to drive a car, and so on – what *is* learning? When do you learn? You learn when you *know* nothing. I learn a language because I do not know it.

56

Right? If I already know a language I can't learn it! Let us experiment with this. Are we learning now – that is, in the active present – or are we only accumulating what has been said, to be stored up and thought about later? Do you see the difference?

We have been talking about dreams. I want to learn about myself, the 'myself' that dreams. Now, do I approach it with the knowledge I have acquired by reading Jung or Freud, or the theologians?

*Questioner: From reading Freud you learn about Freud.*

KRISHNAMURTI: That's it, sir. I learn about Freud: I do not learn about myself. Therefore when I learn through Freud about myself I am not observing myself; I am observing the image which Freud has created about me. So I have to get rid of Freud. Now, please go slowly with this: as I look at myself I am learning about myself. Do I accumulate the knowledge about myself and then, with that knowledge, observe? – which is the same process as looking at myself through Freud. Do you follow? So can I learn about myself – but without any accumulation? That is the *only* way to learn, because the 'myself' is always moving, all the time tremendously active, and I cannot learn about this activity through something static, whether it be the knowledge I have accumulated about myself or the knowledge from Freud. Therefore I have to be free, not only of Freud but also free of the knowledge I have gathered about myself yesterday. It is very complicated – and it is not just a trick.

*Questioner: It seems you set aside knowledge and learn about facts?*

KRISHNAMURTI: That's it. That is, when you observe the fact *without* knowledge, then you can learn. Otherwise you 'know', or think you know. So learning then is creative; it is something new. All the time you are learning. So I have to throw away not only Freud and Jung, but also the knowledge which I have acquired about myself yesterday. Is that possible, first?

*Questioner: You include yesterday, sir. And there are those millions of yesterdays which we have forgotten consciously, but which are in our subconscious. All that has to be got rid of too, has it not?*

KRISHNAMURTI: Yes. Can you get rid of it?

*Questioner: I think it can be got rid of . . .*

KRISHNAMURTI: You *think* it can – therefore you don't *know*. All you can say is that you do not know. Now, go slowly; listen quietly. Please inquire into the state of the mind that says: 'I do not know.'

*Questioner: It is quiet.*

*Questioner: It is open.*

KRISHNAMURTI: No, no! Don't just make statements. Just look. There are two million years of inheritance, thousands and thousands of experiences, impressions, conditions, knowledge. All that is my background, and I want to learn about it, open it all up and be free of it, because those things are controlling my present and shaping the future, and so I continue to live in a cage. So I say to myself: 'This is terrible. I must get rid of it.' I do not know what to do. *I do not know.* Then I ask myself: what is the state of my mind when I say I really do not know? You and I are the result of two million years of conditioning. Right? In that two million years there is not only the animal inheritance but the human endeavour to grow, to become – hundreds of things. We are *that.* And all that is operating in the present and the future. This is the rat race I have lived in. So I look at this rat race, and I say: 'I must get rid of it.' I ask you about it, and you do not know: I ask the Pope, dozens of people, and they do not know. They know only according to their terminology; that is, if you believe in Jesus, if you believe in God, you think you know according to that. So I am now in a position to find out what is the state of my mind when I say: I really do not know. Do you ever say that?

*Questioner: It is a very fine experience, actually.*

*Questioner: It is a humbling experience.*

KRISHNAMURTI: No, no! It is not an experience at all. I do not call it an experience. It is not a sad or a great experience; it is a *fact*. I cannot say it is good or bad. It is a fact – like this microphone. I have looked north, south, east and west, up and down, and I really do not know. Then what happens?

*Questioner: You keep seeking a way.*

KRISHNAMURTI: Then you are no longer saying: I do not know.

*Questioner: I do not know how.*

KRISHNAMURTI: Then you are seeking the 'how'. I am caught in a trap of two million years. I cannot have faith in anybody – the saviours, the masters, the teachers, the priests – because they have all led me into this trap, and I am part of this trap. I do not know how to get out. When I say, 'I do not know,' do I really mean that, or am I looking for a way out?

*Questioner: I mean there is no answer in the catalogue.*

KRISHNAMURTI: That is all. Your catalogue has no answer, and therefore you want to find another catalogue that has an answer.

*Questioner: You keep on trying to find a way.*

KRISHNAMURTI: Then you are back in the trap. Sirs, we have said: 'I do not know.' Our minds are confused, and out of that confusion we seek the priests, the psychologists, the politicians. The confusion creates more confusion. Why don't I say: 'All right, I am confused. I will not act.' Of course I will go to the office, continue with everyday activities, but over my psychological confusion I will not do

59

anything, because I see that if I do anything it will create more confusion. Therefore, psychologically, I will not move at all. Any movement leads to the trap. So can you psychologically do nothing about the trap?

Please listen carefully. If you do nothing about the trap you are free of it. It is only the incessant activity of doing something *about* the trap that keeps you in the trap. When you see that is so, you will stop, won't you? You will cease all activity. And what does that mean? It means that you are willing psychologically to die. So when you do not know, and you really mean it, you are out of the trap, because the past has come to an end. It is when you continually say, 'I am looking, I am asking, I must know,' that the past keeps on repeating itself.

*Questioner: But when you keep silent . . .*

KRISHNAMURTI: Ah! It is not keeping silent. It is the most intense action.

*Questioner: But when you know nothing at all . . .*

KRISHNAMURTI: Then you have *yourself*.

*Questioner: But that is so little.*

KRISHNAMURTI: It is not so little. It is what has been for two million years. It is the most tremendously complex thing, and you have to learn about it. Either you can learn about it instantly, or it can carry on for another two million years. But let us take only fifty years. In that we have accumulated an immense amount: there have been two dreadful wars – the butchery, the brutality, the quarrels, the separations, the insults. It is all there. That is the trap. We are the trap, and so, is it possible to be out of it immediately?

*Questioner: In a moment?*

KRISHNAMURTI: Of course it must be in a moment. And if

you say you cannot, then it is finished. You have no problem. If you say, 'It is possible,' that has no meaning either. But if you say, 'I really don't know what to do,' without despair, without bitterness, without anger, then in that state there is no movement *at all* – then the door opens.

*From* BULLETIN 18, 1973

## Love, Sex and the Religious Life

### KINGSTON, ENGLAND, 2 OCTOBER 1967

I

*Questioner: Many years ago, when I first became interested in the so-called religious life, I made the strong resolve to cut out sex altogether. I conformed rigorously to what I considered to be an essential requirement of that life and lived with all the fierce austerity of a monkish celibate. Now I see that that kind of puritanical conformity in which suppression and violence are involved is stupid, yet I don't want to go back to my old life. How am I to act now in regard to sex?*

KRISHNAMURTI: Why is it that you don't know what to do when there is desire? I'll tell you why. Because this rigid decision of yours is still in operation. All religions have told us to deny sex, to suppress it, because they say it is a waste of energy and you must have energy to find God. But this kind of austerity and harsh suppression and conformity to a pattern does brutal violence to all our finer instincts. This kind of harsh austerity is a greater waste of energy than indulgence in sex.

Why have you made sex into a problem? Really it doesn't matter at all whether you go to bed with someone or

61

whether you don't. Get on with it or drop it but don't make a problem of it. The problem comes from this constant preoccupation. The really interesting thing is not whether we do or don't go to bed with someone but why we have all these fragments in our lives. In one restless corner there is sex with all its preoccupations; in another corner there is some other kind of turmoil; in another a striving after this or that, and in each corner there is the continual chattering of the mind. There are so many ways in which energy is wasted.

If one corner of my life is in disorder, then the whole of my life is in disorder. If there is disorder in my life in regard to sex, then the rest of my life is in disorder. So I shouldn't ask how to put one corner in order, but why I have broken life into so many different fragments – fragments which are in disorder within themselves and which all contradict each other. What can I do when I see so many fragments? How can I deal with them all? I have these fragments because I am not whole inside. If I go into all this without causing yet another fragment, if I go to the very end of each fragment, then in that awareness, which is looking, there is no fragmentation. Each fragment is a separate pleasure. I should ask myself whether I am going to stay in some sordid little room of pleasure all my life. Go into the slavery of each pleasure, each fragment, and say to yourself, my god, I am dependent, I am a slave to all these little corners – is that all there is to my life? Stay with it and see what happens.

II

*Questioner: I have fallen in love, but I know there is no future to this relationship. It is a situation I have experienced several times before and I don't want to get involved again in all that misery and chaos. Yet I am desperately unhappy without this person. How can I get myself out of this state?*

KRISHNAMURTI: The loneliness, bleakness, wretchedness you feel without this person you love existed before you fell in love. What you call love is merely stimulation, the temporary covering-up of your emptiness. You escaped from loneliness through a person, used this person to cover it up. Your problem is not this relationship but rather it is the problem of your own emptiness. Escape is very dangerous because, like some drug, it hides the real problem. It is because you have no love inside you that you continually look for love to fill you from the outside. This lack of love is your loneliness, and when you see the truth of this you will never again try to fill it with things and people from outside.

There is a difference between understanding the futility of this escape and deciding not to get involved in this kind of relationship. A decision is no good because it strengthens the thing you are deciding against. Understanding is quite different. Decision is suppression, violence, conflict, but to see that there is this loneliness, this emptiness inside yourself and that any action whatever on the part of the observer to change it only strengthens it – that is understanding. Even calling it loneliness is an action of the observer to get rid of it. Such action changes nothing, it merely strengthens the loneliness, but *complete inaction* with regard to this loneliness is change. It is going beyond feeling and thinking, side-stepping them. Whatever is happening inside you – anger, depression, jealousy or any other conflict at all – drop it instantly. Stop it.

### III

*Questioner: Is it possible for a man and woman to live together, to have sex and children, without all the turmoil, bitterness and conflict inherent in such a relationship? Is it possible for there to be freedom on both sides? I don't mean by freedom that the husband or wife should constantly be having affairs with someone else. People usually come together and get married because they fall in love, and in that there is desire, choice, pleasure, possessiveness and tremendous drive. The very nature of this in-loveness is from the start filled with the seeds of conflict.*

KRISHNAMURTI: Is it? Need it be? I very much question that. Can't you fall in love and not have a possessive relationship? I love someone and she loves me and we get married – that is all perfectly straightforward and simple, in that there is no conflict at all. (When I say we get married I might just as well say we decide to live together – don't let's get caught up in words.) Can't one have that without the other, without the tail, as it were, necessarily following? Can't two people be in love and both be so intelligent and so sensitive that there is freedom and absence of a centre that makes for conflict? Conflict is not in the feeling of being in love. The feeling of being in love is utterly without conflict. There is no loss of energy in being in love. The loss of energy is in the tail, in everything that follows – jealousy, possessiveness, suspicion, doubt, the fear of losing that love, the constant demand for reassurance and security. Surely it must be possible to function in a sexual relationship with someone you love without the nightmare which usually follows. Of course it is.

*From* BULLETIN 3, 1969

## A Television Interview

*On 7 December 1970 the BBC televised an interview with Krishnamurti which was filmed in the Krishnamurti School at Brockwood Park Hampshire, earlier in the year. The subjects discussed ranged over a wide field including authority, fear and pleasure, the function of thought, relationship, love and meditation. Extracts from the interview are given below.*

## On Authority

*Interviewer: Mr Krishnamurti, you say all our problems stem from one problem: we live as we are told to live, we are second-hand people, and for centuries we have been submitting to every sort of authority. Now the young today are rebelling against authority. What have you personally against authority?*

KRISHNAMURTI: I don't think I have anything personally against authority, but authority, right throughout the world, has crippled the mind – not only religiously but inwardly – because the authority of a belief imposed by religion surely destroys the discovery of reality. One relies on authority because one is afraid to stand alone.

*Interviewer: I am a little puzzled by this, because surely the accumulated wisdom of the human race is not to be totally thrown away?*

KRISHNAMURTI: No, but what is wisdom? Is wisdom the mere accumulation of knowledge, or does wisdom come only when suffering ends? After all, wisdom isn't in books, nor is it in the accumulated knowledge of others' experience. Surely, wisdom comes in self-understanding, in self-discovery of the whole structure of oneself. In the understanding of oneself is the ending of sorrow and the beginning of wisdom. How can a mind be wise when it is caught up in fear and sorrow? It is only when sorrow – which is fear – ends, that there is a possibility of being wise.

## On Love

*Interviewer: Why is it we all so desperately want to be loved?*

65

KRISHNAMURTI: Because we are so desperately empty, lonely.

*Interviewer: But you say that loving is more important than being loved.*

KRISHNAMURTI: Yes, of course – which means one must understand this emptiness, this loneliness in oneself. A mind that is self-concerned with its own ambitions, greeds, fears, guilt, suffering has no capacity to love. A mind that is divided in itself, that lives in fragments, obviously cannot love. Division implies sorrow; it is the root cause of sorrow – division between 'you' and 'me', 'we' and 'they', the black, the white, the brown and so on. So wherever there is division, fragmentation, love cannot be, because goodness is a state of non-division. The world itself is indivisible.

*Interviewer: You say, in fact, that love can only come into being when there is a total self-abandonment. But how does one achieve self-abandonment?*

KRISHNAMURTI: Total abandonment can only happen with the understanding of oneself. Self-knowledge is the beginning of wisdom and therefore wisdom and love go together. This means there is love only when I have really understood myself and therefore know in myself there is no fragmentation at all – no sense of anger, ambition, greed, separative activity.

*Interviewer: But, you see, we have still to live in society and a rather sick society at that, and this impinges on us: we're not really free to be ourselves partly because of the society.*

KRISHNAMURTI: But surely, sir, we *are* the society. We have built the society – the society is us, the world is us. It's not that the world is something different from me. I am the result of the world, of the society, the culture, the religion, the environment in which I have lived.

66

*Interviewer: You said, you see, that it is effort that destroys us, that life is a series of battles, and the only happy man is one who is not caught up in effort. But, can you do any work in the world without some hard effort?*

KRISHNAMURTI: Why not sir? But what is effort? It is a contradiction of energies, isn't it? One energy opposing another energy.

*Interviewer: Couldn't it be a steadfast drive in one direction?*

KRISHNAMURTI: If there is one drive, one pursuit, where is the contradiction in that? There is no wastage of energy, no conflict. If I go for a walk, I go for a walk. But if I want to go out for a walk and yet I have to do something else, then the contradiction begins, then conflict, then effort. So that's why, to understand effort, one has to find out how contradictory we are.

## On Meditation

*Interviewer: What do you mean by meditation? The word occurs often in your books. I looked it up in the Oxford Dictionary before coming to see you and it says meditation means indulging in thought. But you don't want us to do this.*

KRISHNAMURTI: One has to go into this to know what it really means – for me it is one of the most important things.

*Interviewer: Could it best be explained by your telling me what it is not?*

KRISHNAMURTI: I was just going to suggest that. You see, there are various schools of meditation. They offer various systems, methods, and they say that if you practise these methods day after day, you will achieve a certain form of enlightenment, a certain extraordinary experience. First of all, the whole idea of systems, methods, implies mechanical

67

repetition – and that is not meditation. Now, is it possible not to make the mind dull by repetition, but to be aware of this movement of thought – without suppression, without trying to control thoughts, but just to be aware of this whole momentum of thinking, this chattering going on?

*Interviewer: But we verbalize our thoughts all the time, don't we?*

KRISHNAMURTI: That's it. Thought exists only in words, or in images. Meditation demands the most extraordinary discipline – not the discipline of suppression and conformity – but that which comes when you observe your thinking, when there is an observation of thought. That very observation brings its own extraordinary subtle discipline. That is absolutely necessary.

*Interviewer: Does one set aside time for this?*

KRISHNAMURTI: Sir, you can do it at any time. You can do it when you are sitting in a bus – that is, watch, observe. Be attentive to what is happening around you and what is happening in yourself – aware of the whole movement. You see, meditation is really a form of emptying the mind of everything known. Without this, you cannot know the unknown. To see anything new, totally new, the mind must be empty of all the past. Truth, or God, or whatever name you like to give to it must be new, not something which is the result of propaganda, the result of conditioning. The Christian is conditioned by 2,000 years of propaganda, the Hindu, the Buddhist likewise conditioned. So for them God or Truth is the result of propaganda. But that is not Truth. Truth is something living every day. Therefore the mind must be emptied to look at Truth.

*Interviewer: You wipe the slate clean, so to speak?*

KRISHNAMURTI: That is meditation.

*Interviewer: And then you get this total, relaxed perception of 'what is'.*

KRISHNAMURTI: Of 'what is' – that's right. And 'what is' is not a static thing; it is extraordinarily alive. And therefore the mind that is really in meditation, the meditative mind, is a very silent mind, and the silence is not the product of suppression of noise. It is not the opposite of noise. It comes when the mind has completely understood itself – therefore no movement at all takes place, which means the brain cells themselves become quiet. And then in that silence everything happens. This is an extraordinary thing, if one has observed it. That is real meditation, not all this phoney acceptance of authority and repetition of words, and all that business. That's all nonsense.

*Interviewer: May I try to recapitulate, and you tell me if I have misunderstood? Meditation, it seems to me, is the essential unconditioning process.*

KRISHNAMURTI: That's right.

*Interviewer: And if I discard this dead weight of authority, if I discard everything I've been told, I shall be totally alone at that moment, but in that solitude there's a chance I may understand what I really am.*

KRISHNAMURTI: And what Truth is, or God, or whatever name you like to give it.

*From* BULLETIN 9, 1970–71

## The Capacity to Listen

SANTA MONICA, CALIFORNIA, MARCH 1974

*Questioner: I have been listening to you for some time now, but no change has come about.*

KRISHNAMURTI: 'I have been listening for some years to your talks and no change has come about in me.' Then don't listen any more.

Now look, sir, if you listen to somebody for years, and you see for yourself the beauty of what is being said, then you want to listen more; then it opens doors to you which you have never seen before. But if it doesn't, then what is wrong? What is wrong with the speaker who says these things, or what is wrong with the listener? Why is it that a man or woman who has heard the speaker for many years is not changed? In that there is great sorrow, is there not?

You see a flower, a lovely flower by the wayside, you glance and pass by. You don't stop to look, you don't see the beauty, the quiet dignity, the loveliness. You pass by. What is wrong? Is it that you are not serious? Is it that you don't care? Is it that you have so many problems that you are caught up in them, no time, no leisure to stop, so that you never look at that flower? Or is it that what the speaker is saying has no value in itself – not what you think about it – but in itself it has no value? Has it no value? To determine whether it has or has not, you have to investigate what the speaker is saying. And to investigate you must have the capacity to listen, you must be able to look, you must give your time to it. So is it your responsibility or is it the responsibility of the speaker? It is our mutual responsibility, isn't it? Both of us have to look. The speaker may point out, but you have to look, you have to go into it, you have to learn. And if your mind is not diligent but negligent, if your mind is not watching, highly sensitive, it is your doing. That means you have to change your ways of life; everything has to be changed to learn a way of living which is entirely different. And that demands energy; you cannot be lazy, indolent.

So since it is our mutual responsibility – maybe more yours than that of the speaker – perhaps, sir, you have not given your life to it. We are talking about life – not about ideas, not about theories, practices, not even techniques – but to look at this whole life, which is your life, and to care for it. And that means not to waste your life. You have a very short time to live, maybe ten, maybe fifty years, but don't waste it. Look at it, give your life to understand it.

*From* BULLETIN 27, 1975

## An Investigation into Friendship

SANTA MONICA, CALIFORNIA (UNDATED)

*Questioner: What is real friendship, if there is no trust and respect?*

KRISHNAMURTI: Without trust and respect, how can you have friendship? I really don't know! But, look, sir, first of all why do you want a friend? Is it because you want to depend on him, rely on him, have companionship? It is out of your loneliness, insufficiency that you depend on another to fill that emptiness and therefore you are using another, exploiting another to cover your own insufficiency, your own emptiness, and so call that person a friend? Is he a friend in that way – using him for your pleasure, your comfort and so on? Go into it, sir, don't accept what I am saying. Most of us are so lonely, and the older we get the more lonely we feel and discover our own emptiness.

When you are young these things don't occur to you. But as you grow to maturity – if you are ever mature at all – then you discover for yourself what it means to be empty, lonely, to have no friend at all because you have led a superficial life, depended on others, exploited others. You have invested your heart, your feelings in others, and when they die, or go away you feel so lonely, empty: and out of

71

that emptiness there is self-pity, and you dream of finding somebody to fill that emptiness. This is what is happening all the days of our life.

Now, can you see this and learn about it? Learn what it means to be lonely and never escape from it. Look at it, live with it, see what is implied, so that psychologically, inwardly, you depend on nobody. Then you will know what it means to love.

*From* BULLETIN 30, 1976

## *What is Beauty?*

LONDON, ENGLAND (UNDATED)

*Questioner: I don't know what beauty is. I never even thought about it until I heard you talk about it. I'm an engineer and have constructed many buildings, bridges and railways. I've lived a hard life in the open and in countries where there are few trees. On a walk one day you pointed out the beautiful shape of a tree. I looked at it and repeated the words, 'How beautiful,' but deeply inside me I didn't really feel anything at all. I politely agreed with you, but I don't really know what beauty is. Sometimes a straight railway line might seem beautiful to me and sometimes I admire one of those marvellous modern bridges across a great river or across the mouth of a harbour. They are functional and are supposed to be quite beautiful, but I don't really see it. Those modern jet planes are functional machines. When you pointed them out to me and said they were beautiful I somehow felt they were things to be used and wondered why you got so excited about them. That yellow flower on the walk didn't give me at all the same quality of feeling as it gave you. I dare say I am rather crude. Your mind is much sharper than mine. I've never bothered to look at my feelings or cultivate them. I've had children and the pleasure of sex, but even that has been rather dull and heavy. And now I wonder if I am not being deprived of something which you call beauty and whether at my age I can ever really feel it, see the world as a marvellous thing, the heavens, the woods and the rivers. What is beauty?*

KRISHNAMURTI: Are you talking about the beauty of living or the beauty that the eye sees in something, or the beauty of a poem or the beauty of music? Probably all this may sound to you rather sentimental and emotional, but there is beauty in mathematics too, which you know. In that there is supreme order. And isn't the same order in life also beautiful?

*Questioner: I don't know if it is beautiful, but I do know what I've done with my own life: I've rigorously, almost brutally, disciplined myself, and there is a certain tortured order in that. But probably you would say that this is not order at all. I don't really know what it means to live beautifully. In fact, I really know nothing except a few mechanical things connected with my job; I see by talking to you that my life is pretty dull, or rather my mind is. So how can I wake up to this sensitivity, to this intelligence that makes life extremely beautiful to you?*

KRISHNAMURTI: First, sir, one has to sharpen the senses by looking, touching, observing, listening not only to the birds, to the rustle of the leaves, but also to the words that you use yourself, the feeling you have — however small and petty — for all the secret intimations of your own mind. Listen to them and don't suppress them, don't control them or try to sublimate them. Just listen to them. The sensitivity to the senses doesn't mean their indulgence, doesn't mean yielding to urges or resisting those urges, but means simply observing so that the mind is always watchful as when you walk on a railway line; you may lose your balance but you immediately get back on to the rail. So the whole organism becomes alive, sensitive, intelligent, balanced, taut.

73

Probably you consider the body is not at all important. I've seen you eat, and you eat as if you were feeding a furnace. You may like the taste of food, but it is all so mechanical, so inattentive, the way you mix food on your plate. When you become aware of all this, your fingers, your eyes, your ears, your body all become sensitive, alive, responsive. This is comparatively easy. But what is more difficult is to free the mind from the mechanical habits of thought, feeling and action into which it has been driven by circumstances – by one's wife, one's children, one's job. The mind itself has lost its elasticity. The more subtle forms of observation escape it. This means seeing yourself actually as you are without wanting to correct yourself or change what you see or escape from it – just to see yourself actually as you are, so that the mind doesn't fall back into another series of habits. When such a mind looks at a flower or the colour of a dress or a dead leaf falling from a tree, it is now capable of seeing the movement of that leaf as it falls and the colour of that flower vividly. So both outwardly and inwardly the mind becomes highly alive, pliable, alert; there is a sensitivity which makes the mind intelligent. Sensitivity, intelligence and freedom in action are the beauty of living.

*Questioner: All right. So one observes, one becomes very sensitive, very watchful, and then what? Is that all there is, just marvelling forever at perfectly commonplace things? I am sure that everybody does this all the time, at least when they are young, and there is nothing earth-shaking about it. What then? Isn't there some further step than just this observation that you talk about?*

KRISHNAMURTI: You started this conversation by asking about beauty, by saying that you do not feel it. You also said that in your life there is no beauty and so we are inquiring into this question of what beauty is, not only verbally or intellectually but feeling the very throb of it.

*Questioner: Yes, that is so, but when I asked you I wondered if there isn't something beyond just the sensitive looking you describe.*

74

KRISHNAMURTI: Of course there is, but unless one has the sensitivity of observation, seeing what is infinitely greater cannot come about.

*Questioner: So many people do see with heightened sensitivity. Poets look with intense feeling, yet in all this there doesn't seem to be any breakthrough to that infinitely greater, infinitely more beautiful something which people call the divine. Because I feel that whether one is very sensitive or rather dull, as I am, unless there is a breakthrough to some quite different dimension what we perceive is simply varying shades of grey. In all this sensitivity which you say comes about through observation it seems to me there is just a quantitative difference, just a small improvement, not something really vastly different. Frankly I am not interested in just a little more of the same thing.*

KRISHNAMURTI: So what are you asking now? Are you asking how to break through the dull grey monotony of life to some quite different dimension?

*Questioner: Yes. Real beauty must be something other than the beauty of the poet, the artist, the young, alert mind, though I am not in any way belittling that beauty.*

KRISHNAMURTI: Is this really what you are seeking? Is it really what you want? If you do, there must be the total revolution of your being. Is this what you want? Do you want a revolution that shatters all your concepts, your values, your morality, your respectability, your knowledge – shatters you so that you are reduced to absolute nothingness, so that you no longer have any character, so that you no longer are the seeker, the man who judges, who is aggressive or perhaps non-aggressive, so that you are completely empty of everything that is you? This emptiness is beauty with its extreme austerity in which there is not a spark of harshness or aggressive assertion. This is what breaking through means, and is this what you are after? There must be an astonishing intelligence, not information or learning. This intelligence operates all the time, whether you are asleep or awake. That is why we said there must be the observation of the outer and the inner which sharpens the brain. And this very sharpness of the brain makes it quiet. And it is this sensitivity and intelligence that make thought operate only when it has to; the rest of the time the brain is not dormant but watchfully quiet. And so the brain with its reactions doesn't bring about conflict. It functions without struggle and therefore without distortion. Then the doing and the acting are immediate, as when you see danger. Therefore there is always a freedom from conceptual accumulations. It is this conceptual accumulation which is the observer, the ego, the 'me' which divides, resists and builds barriers. When the 'me' is not, the breakthrough is not, then there is no breakthrough; then the whole of life is in the beauty of living, the beauty of relationship, without substituting one image for another. Then only the infinitely greater is possible.

*From* BULLETIN 32, 1977

## Freedom from Attachments

SAANEN, SWITZERLAND, 16 JULY 1974

*Questioner: I see the implications of attachment, but nevertheless I would like to ask if there isn't a certain biological attachment? There are attachments in the animal kingdom. How can you possibly visualize the human race, composed of millions of people, human families, with no attachments among themselves?*

KRISHNAMURTI: Wait, sir. Are we talking to the millions of people about attachment, or are we talking to you about attachment? You understand my question? Because the millions of people are not concerned with this. The millions of India, South America and so on are not concerned with this. They say, 'For god's sake give me food, clothing and shelter – I am starving, I am diseased.' And you are saying, 'How can you ask these millions of people to be detached?' You can't! But we are talking to you – right? Please listen to this: if in your consciousness, which is the consciousness of millions of people, there is a transformation, then that transformation affects the millions. Then you will have a different kind of education, a different kind of society, do you follow?

You are attached to your mother, of course. When you are a child you need a mother and a father to look after you; the child needs complete security, the more security of the right kind the happier he is. But millions of people want security, and they think they will find it in attachment, to their country, to their little house. They are willing to fight the rest of the world for their country, this is their attachment. The Catholic is willing to fight the Protestant for his attachment. Now we are concerned with the people who are in this tent for the moment. If I went and talked to people labouring on the road they would say, 'Please go away, what we need is some beer.' We are talking to you. Can you change the content of your consciousness so that in that transformation you affect the consciousness of man? Look, the so-called religions have talked to individuals for thousands of years and your consciousness has accepted this conditioning as Catholics or Protestants, and you function from there if you are at all serious in what you have been conditioned to, and your consciousness has affected the consciousness of the world. Now we are saying: in the transformation of your consciousness, with all its content, in that freedom you have tremendous energy, which is the essence of intelligence and that intelligence will operate in every field if you are aware of the total human existence.

See what is happening: everybody needs clothes, food and shelter, but that is prevented by the division, the radical division, national division, economic division, the competition for power among the nations. Once we were talking about this to a prominent politician, a member of the Cabinet, and he said, 'My dear man, that is impossible, a marvellous ideal, but far away in the distance; I like what you say, but it is impracticable. We have to deal with the immediate.' You follow? And the immediate is their power, their position, their ideology, the most impracticable and the most destructive thing. You know all this. Do you mean to say that if all the politicians in the world got together and said, 'Look, forget your systems, forget your ideologies, forget your power, let us be concerned with human suffering, human needs, food, clothing, shelter' – do you mean to say that we could not solve this problem? Of course we could. But nobody wants to. Everybody is concerned with his own immediate sickness and ideology.

*From* BULLETIN 32, 1977

## If One is the World

OJAI, CALIFORNIA, 13 MAY 1980

*Questioner: If one is the world, what does it mean to step out of the stream, and 'who' steps out of it?*

KRISHNAMURTI: I wonder if one realizes, not as an idea, not as something of romantic appeal, but as an actual fact, that one is the world – psychologically, inwardly, one is the world. Go to India, they have the same problems as here, suffering, loneliness, death, anxiety, sorrow. Wherever one goes this is the fact common to humanity.

78

When you hear this statement that psychologically, inwardly, one is the world, do you make of it an idea? Or do you actually realize it as you realize it when a pin is thrust into your thigh or your arm, the actual pain of it? You don't have an idea about that: it is so, there is pain. So does one actually realize that immense fact, feel it as something vital, something that is tremendously actual? If one does, then that psychological fact affects the mind, the brain – not one's little mind narrowed by national or family concerns – it affects the human brain. When one realizes that, it brings a sense of great responsibility, without any sense of guilt, but a sense of tremendous responsibility for all things connected with human beings, how one educates one's children, how one behaves, and so on. If one actually realizes this immensity – it is immense – then the particular entity as 'me' seems so insignificant; all one's little worries become so shoddy.

When one sees this fact, when it is felt in one's heart and mind, one covers the earth; one wants to protect everything, for one is responsible.

The questioner asks: What does it mean to step out of this stream and 'who' steps out of it? The stream is the constant struggle and misery of all human beings, whether communist, socialist or imperialist: it is the common ground on which we all stand. To be free of that, there is no 'who' that steps out of it; the mind has become something totally different. It is not: 'I step out of it'; the mind is no longer in it.

If you are attached and you end attachment, something totally different takes place; it is not that you are free from attachment. There is a different quality, a different tone to one's whole life when one realizes this tremendous fact, that we are humanity.

*From* BULLETIN 40, 1981

79

# *Aggression*

OJAI, CALIFORNIA, 15 MAY 1980

*Questioner: In observation without the observer, is there a transformation from staying with the fact that leads to increase of attention? Does the energy created have a direction?*

KRISHNAMURTI: These questions unfortunately do not relate to actual life. That is not to say one should not put these questions, but have they actually touched one's daily life? Such questions as these are theoretical, abstract, something one has heard about. Why not look at one's life and find out why one lives this way, why one is worried, why one's mind is eternally chattering, why one has no right relationship with another, why one is cruel? Why is one's mind so narrow, why is one neurotic? Apparently one never deals with questions that affect one's daily existence. I wonder why? If one asks a really genuine question that deeply affects one's life, it has much more vitality.

So I will ask a question: why do we, each one of us, live the way we are living, taking drugs, drinking, smoking, pursuing pleasure and aggression? Why are we like that? Why are we aggressive? In the whole of the society in which we live aggression is one of the most important things, and competition – they go together. You can see aggression in animals in certain seasons, in mating. But at other times they do not compete. A lion kills a zebra, other lions share it. But apparently with us aggression is a most deep-rooted thing.

Why do we compete? Is it the fault of this society, of our education? Do not blame society for this; society is what we have made it, and if one is not competitive, not aggressive, then in this society one is trodden down, discarded, looked down upon.

Are we aggressive because of the emphasis on individual freedom, a freedom that demands that one must express oneself at any cost, especially in the West? There is a belief that if one wants to do something, one does it; do not refrain, do not examine it, it does not matter; if one has an urge, one must act. One can see what aggression does. One is aggressive, competing for the same job, for this, that or the other, fighting each other all along the way, both psychologically and physically.

That is the pattern in which one carries on, part of one's social education. And to break that pattern it is said one must exercise will. Exercising one's will is another form of 'I must', another form of aggression. One is aggressive, that has been the pattern from childhood imprinted by the mother, the father, by education and society, and from the boys around who are all aggressive. And one likes that, it gives pleasure, one accepts it and so one also becomes aggressive. Then, as one grows up, somebody shows one the nature of aggression, what it does in society, how competition is destroying human beings. Not only does the speaker say this, but scientists are beginning to say it – so perhaps one will accept what the scientists say. It is explained to one carefully, the reason, the cause, the destructive nature of competition, and of always comparing. Now the mind that does not compare at all is a totally different kind of mind; it has much more vitality.

So all this is explained to one, and yet one goes on being aggressive, competitive, comparing oneself with others, always striving for something much greater – not for the lesser, but always the greater. So there is this pattern established, this framework, in which the mind is caught.

One listens to this and says, 'I must get out of it, I must do something about it,' which is another form of aggression.

So can one have an insight into aggression? – not the remembrance of the implications of it, which means constant examination, coming to a conclusion and acting according to that conclusion – that is not insight. But if one has an immediate insight into it, then one has broken the whole pattern of aggression.

So what will you do about the way you are living: the everlasting going to meetings, discussions with philosophers, and the latest psychologists? One never says, 'Look, I am like this, let me find out why. Why does one have wounds, psychological bruises? Why does one live with them?'

But, really, somebody who has been attending Krishnamurti's talks for fifty years and more, and knows all this by heart, does not have to quote me. Do not quote; find out for yourself, then there is greater energy and you become much more alive.

*From* BULLETIN 40, 1981

## Will and Desire

SAANEN, SWITZERLAND, 23 JULY 1980

*Questioner: Without the operation of desire and will, how does one move in the direction of self-knowledge? Is not the very urgency to change, a part of the movement of desire? What is the nature of the first step?*

KRISHNAMURTI: To understand this question, not just superficially but in depth, one must understand the nature of desire and will, and also the nature of self-knowing. The questioner asks: if one has not the urge, which is part of desire and will, how can the flowering take place in knowing oneself?

What is the relationship of desire to will? How does desire come into being? First there are the visual and tactile sensations; then thought creates an image out of those sensations, and desire is born. One can see this for oneself when looking in a shop window at a shirt or a dress; on entering the shop, the tactile sensation is aroused in touching the material, and then thought says, 'How nice to have that dress!' Thought creates the image of putting on the dress and at that moment desire arises. This is the movement; perception, contact, sensation – quite natural, healthy – then thought takes possession of sensation, creates an image, and desire is born. Will is the summation of desire, the strengthening of desire, the urge to achieve, to express one's desire, and acquire; it is the operation of desire strengthened by will.

So desire and will go together. Now the questioner asks: 'If there is no desire or will, why should one seek self-knowledge?' What is self-knowledge? Let us examine that first. The ancient Greeks and the Hindus talked about knowing oneself. What does it mean, to know oneself? Can one ever know oneself? What *is* the self that, apparently, it is necessary to know? And what does one mean by the word 'know'? I know Gstaad* because I have come here for twenty-two years. I know you because I have seen you here for twenty years or more. When one says, 'I know', one means by that, not only recognition but also remembrance of the face, the name. There is association: 'I met you yesterday, I recognize you today.' That is the memory operating. So when one says, 'I know,' it is the past expressing itself in the present. One goes to school, college, university and acquires a great deal of knowledge. Then one says, 'I am a chemist, or a physicist,' or this and that. So when one says one must know oneself, does one come to know about the self afresh, or does one approach it from a base of knowledge already

*The resort near Saanen where Krishnamurti stayed.

acquired? You see the difference?

I want to know myself. I may have studied psychology, or been to psychotherapists, or read a great deal. Do I approach the understanding of the self through that knowledge? Or do I come to it without the previous accumulation of knowledge about myself. When I say, 'I must know about myself', am I not already acquainted with myself through past knowledge which dictates how I observe myself? It is very important to understand this if one wants to go into it carefully. So, having previous knowledge about oneself, one uses that knowledge to understand oneself; which is absurd. So can one put aside all that one has understood about oneself from the knowledge of others – Freud, Jung, the modern psychologists – and look at oneself afresh, anew?

Now the questioner asks: are desire and will necessary in observing myself? See what happens. One has acquired knowledge about oneself through others as opposed to the actual fact of what one is. You see the difference? There is a contradiction between what I have acquired and 'what is'. And to overcome this contradiction one exercises will. One may have gone to the latest psychotherapist and been given by him certain knowledge about oneself; that knowledge one takes home and discovers that it is different from what one is. Then begins the conflict: to adjust what I have been told to 'what is'. To overcome that conflict, to suppress it, or accept it, desire and will come into being.

Now, are will and desire necessary at all? Do they not come into being only when one has to adjust oneself to a pattern, to a pattern of 'good'? Then does not the conflict, the struggle to overcome, to control, begin?

One is a seeker, one is questioning; therefore one rejects completely all information provided by others about oneself. Will one do that? One will not, because it is much safer to accept authority. Then one feels secure. But if one does completely reject the authority of everybody, how does one observe the movement of the self, for the self is not static, it is moving, living, acting? How does one observe something that is tremendously active, full of urges, desires, ambitions, greed, romanticism? Which means: can one observe the movement of the self with all its desires and fears, without knowledge acquired from others or which one has acquired in examining oneself?

One of the activities of the self is greed. Now, when one uses the word 'greed', one has already associated that reaction, or that reflex, with a memory one has previously had of that reaction. One uses the word 'greed' to identify that sensation, to recognize it, and the moment that recognition takes place, it is already strengthened and taken back into memory. So can one look at that sensation, that reaction, without the word, and therefore without the previous acquaintance with it? Can one look at that reaction without a single movement of recognition?

Now, can one observe oneself without any direction, without any comparison and therefore without motive? That is learning about oneself afresh each time. If one goes very seriously into this, one will find that it is not a matter of little by little, first one step, then another, but of seeing the truth of it instantly, the truth that the moment recognition takes place one is not knowing oneself at all. It requires a great deal of attention to do this, and most of us are so slack, so lazy; we have all kinds of ideas about what we should or should not be, so we come to it with a tremendous burden and therefore never know ourselves.

To put it differently: we are like the rest of mankind, and mankind, throughout the entire world, suffers, goes through great misery, uncertainty, sorrow. So, psychologically, one is like the rest of humanity; one is humanity. Then the problem arises: can the content of one's consciousness be wiped away, all the learning about oneself, which is the consciousness of mankind? One is so conditioned to the idea of oneself as an individual, psychologically different from another –

which is not a fact – that when one says, 'I must know myself,' one is saying 'I must know my little cell' – and when one investigates that little cell, it is nothing. But the actual truth is that one is mankind, one is the rest of humanity. To inquire into the enormous complex of the human mind is to read the story of oneself. One is history, and if one knows how to read the book, one begins to find out the nature of oneself, the nature of this consciousness which is the consciousness of all human beings.

*From* BULLETIN 40, SPRING AND SUMMER 1981

# Where Knowledge is not Needed

SAANEN, SWITZERLAND, 29 JULY 1981

*Questioner: How does one draw the dividing line between knowledge that must be retained and that which is to be abandoned? What is it that makes the decision?*

KRISHNAMURTI: The questioner is asking where to draw the line between retaining knowledge which is necessary to become an engineer, a carpenter or a plumber, and recording personal knowledge, personal hurts, personal ambitions where apparently we have retained knowledge with resultant harm. So where do you draw the line between that and this, and the questioner asks: what is it that makes the decision?

Do you see one of the factors in this question – how we all depend on decisions? I will decide to go here, not there. What is that decision based on? Just look carefully: on pleasure – my past knowledge, past pleasure or past pain, past remembrance of things, which says, 'Don't do that any more,' or 'Do it.' That is, in decision there is the element of will. Will is the accumulated, concentrated form of desire. Right? Desire, which says, 'I must do that,' but I call it 'will'. We have already been into the question of desire, so I won't go into it now. We are saying that will is a great element in decision, and on that tradition we are conditioned. We are questioning that action because will, which is essentially desire, is a divisive factor: the will to succeed, the will to do something and my wife is against it, the me and the not me, and so on.

So is there a way of living – please listen to this – without the operation of will at all? A way of living in which there is no conflict, as conflict exists as long as I exercise will, obviously. Now let's find out if that is possible.

The questioner asks: how does one draw the line between the factor which accumulates knowledge necessary for skilful action and the non-recording factor of the psyche. Not recording my hurts, insults, flattery, bullying and all that. How does one draw the line between the two? You don't draw the line. The moment you have drawn the line you have made a separation, and therefore you are going to cause conflict between recording and not recording. Then you ask, 'How am I not to record?' I am insulted personally, how can I not record the insult, or the flattery – it is the same thing, flattery and insult are the two sides of the same coin. In the field of technology I must record, and when you insult me my brain instantly records it. Why should I record it? Why should that insult be carried over day after day? And from that insult when I meet you again I retaliate.

Now is it possible not to record at all any psychological factors? You understand my question? My wife, if I have one, says something brutal when I arrive home tired from the office because she has had a tiresome day herself with rumbustious children, so she says something violent. Instantly, because I am tired and I want some kind of peace in the house, I record it. Now I am asking is it possible not to record that incident at all? Otherwise I am building an image about her and she is building an image about me, so the relationship is between images and not between ourselves. So is it possible not to record? The recording process strengthens, gives vitality to a centre which is the 'me'. That is obvious. It is only possible not to record, no matter how tired one is, by being attentive at that moment when the wife or I am brutal, because, as we explained the other day with regard to meditation, where there is attention there is no recording.

So see the truth of this: that on the one level you need knowledge, and here on the other you don't need knowledge at all. See the truth of it – what freedom it brings you. That is real freedom. Right? If you have an insight into it, you don't draw the line nor make a decision. There is no recording.

*From* BULLETIN 45, 1983

# *Do not Ask for Help*

### SAANEN, SWITZERLAND, 30 AUGUST 1981

*Questioner: I have studied, been to Asia, discussed with people there; I have tried to penetrate beyond the superficiality of religions into something I feel in my bones – although I am a logical man – something profoundly mysterious and sacred. And yet I don't seem to apprehend it. Can you help me?*

KRISHNAMURTI: It depends on with whom you have tried to discuss. Shall we go into this question?

One wonders why you go to Asia at all – except for

trade. Perhaps people who go there for religious purposes are in fact trading – you give me something and I will give you something. Is truth there, not here? Is truth to be found through people, through a guru, through a path, a system, through a prophet, a saviour? Or has truth no path?

There is a marvellous Indian story of a boy who leaves home in search of truth. He goes to various teachers, walking endlessly in various parts of the country, every teacher asserting something or other. After many years, as an old man, after searching, searching, asking, meditating, taking certain postures, breathing rightly, fasting, no sex and all that, he comes back to his old house. As he opens the door there it is: the truth is just there. You understand? You might say, 'It wouldn't have been there if he hadn't wandered all over the place.' That's a cunning remark, but you miss the beauty of the story if you don't see that truth is not to be sought after. Truth is not something to be attained, to be experienced, to be held. It is there for those who can see it. But most of us are everlastingly seeking, moving from one fad to another, from one excitement to another excitement, sacrificing – you know all the absurdities that go on – thinking that time will help us to come to truth. Time will not do that.

So the problem is: I am a logical man, yet I feel that something profoundly mysterious exists, but I cannot apprehend it. I can understand it, I can logically see it, but I cannot have it in my heart, in my mind, in my eyes, in my smile. The questioner says, 'Help me.' If one may point out something: don't ask help from anybody, because the whole mystery is in you, the whole travail – if there is a mystery. Everything man has struggled for, sought, found, discarded as illusion, all that is part of your consciousness. When you ask for help – forgive me if I point this out most respectfully, not cynically – when you ask for help you are asking for something from outside, from another. How do you know the other has that quality of truth? Unless you have it yourself you will never know whether he has it or not.

So the first thing is – I am saying this with great affection, with care – please don't ask for help. If you do then the priests, the gurus, the interpreters, all of them smother you with their outpourings. Whereas if you look at the problem, the problem is this: man throughout the ages has sought something sacred, something that is not corrupted by time, by all the travails of thought; he has sought it, longed for it, sacrificed, tortured himself physically, fasted for weeks, but he has not found it. So somebody comes along and says, 'I'll show it to you, I'll help you.' Then you are lost. But when you ask if there is something profoundly mysterious, sacred, the mystery exists only as a concept, but if you uncover it, it is no longer a mystery. Truth isn't a mystery, it is something far beyond all concept of mystery.

So what is one to do? I am human, I can laugh, I can shed tears, but I am a serious man. I have inquired into all the aspects of religion, and I recognize their superficiality, and of the gurus, the churches, the temples, the mosques, the preachers. If I have seen the actual superficiality of one of them, I have seen the whole lot. I don't have to go through them all. So what am I to do? Is there anything to be done? Who is the doer? And what is it that is being done? Please follow all this step by step, if you are interested in it. Can you discard all your superficiality, with your garlands, pictures, all that nonsense? Can you discard all that and stand alone? Because one has to be alone. The word 'alone' means 'all one'. Solitude is one thing, all alone is another. Solitude has in it the quality of loneliness. You can walk in the forest and be alone, or you can walk in the forest feeling that you are in solitude. That feeling is totally different from the feeling of being alone. Now what am I to do? I have meditated, I have followed different systems, practices, and I recognize their superficiality.

I must tell you this story, if you don't mind. We were

speaking in Bombay to an enormous crowd, and the next day a man came to see the speaker. He was an old man, white hair, white beard, and he told me the following story. He had been one of the important judges in India, an advocate, highly placed with a family, children, greatly respected and so on. And one morning he said to himself, 'I pass judgement on others, criminals, swindlers, robbers, embezzlers, businessmen and politicians, but I don't know what truth is. How can I pass judgement if I don't know what truth is?' And so he withdrew, withdrew from his family and went into the forest to meditate. That is one of the old traditions in India, highly regarded to this day, that when a man renounces the world, wherever he wanders in India, he must be clothed, fed, respected. It is not an organized society of monks. He is alone. So he withdrew to a forest, and he told me that he had been meditating for twenty-five years. Now, after hearing the speaker the previous evening, he said, 'I have come to say how deeply I have hypnotized myself, how in this hypnosis I have deceived myself.' For a man who has meditated for twenty-five years to acknowledge that he has deceived himself – you understand the nature of a human being who admits that?

So here am I, serious, having a certain amount of leisure, not following anybody – because if you follow anybody that is the end of it. Please see this. It is the end of your penetration into that which is eternal. You have to be completely a light to yourself. I realize that so I don't follow anybody or any worship, any ritual, and yet that which is eternal is eluding me. It is not in my breath, in my eyes, in my heart. So what am I to do?

First of all can the brain be free of the centre, which is me? You understand my question? Can my brain be free of myself, the self? Whether that self is a super or ultra super self, it is still the self. Is there total dissipation of selfishness – to put it very simply? The self centre is very cunning – it can think it has escaped from all selfishness, from all concern about its own entity, its own becoming, and yet very subtly, deeply, it is putting out a tentacle. So one has to discover for oneself whether there can be complete and total freedom from all selfishness, which is all self-centred activity. That is meditation – to find out a way of living in this world without being selfish, self-centred, without egocentric activity, egocentric movement. If there is a shadow of that, a movement of that, then you are lost. So one has to be tremendously aware of every movement of thought.

That is very easy, don't complicate it. At the moment when you are angry you do not even know that feeling. But when you examine it, you can observe the arising of it, the arising of greed, of envy, of ambition, of aggression. As it arises watch it – not after it is over – you understand? As it arises, as you watch it, it withers away. So the brain can be aware of the arising of thought, and that awareness of the arising of thought is attention. Do not smother it, destroy it, put it away, but just be aware of the feeling. Don't you know the feeling of hunger when it arises, or your sexual feeling? Obviously you do. As it arises be completely aware of it and with that awareness, that attention to the movement of the me', my desire, my ambition, my egotistic pursuit wither away. That awareness is absolutely necessary so that there is not a particle, a shadow of this 'me', because the 'me' is separate. We have been into all that. So that is the first thing you have to understand – not control of the body, special breathing, yoga; wash your hands of all that. Then you have a brain that is not acting partially, but wholly.

We pointed out the other day that we are functioning not with all our senses, but only partially. The partiality, the narrowness, emphasizes the self, of course. I am not going to go into it in detail; you can see it for yourself. When you observe the mountain, the trees, the river, the blue sky, the person whom you love with all your senses, there is no self. There is no 'me' that is feeling all this, and that means a brain that is not functioning as a dentist, or a scholar, or a labourer, or an astronomer, but a brain that is functioning as a whole. That can take place only when the brain is completely quiet, so there is no shadow of the self, absolute silence of the mind – not emptiness, that conveys a wrong meaning. Most people's brains are empty anyhow. But only a brain that is not occupied with anything, including God, is silent, full of vitality, and that brain has a great sense of love, compassion, which is intelligence.

*From* BULLETIN 47, 1984

## The Aim of the Krishnamurti Schools

BROCKWOOD PARK, ENGLAND, 1 SEPTEMBER 1981

*Questioner: You have often said no one can show the way to truth. Yet your schools are said to help their members to understand themselves. Is this not a contradiction? Does it not create an élite atmosphere?*

KRISHNAMURTI: The speaker has said that there is no path to truth, that no one can lead another to it. He has repeated this very often for the last sixty years. And the speaker with the help of others has founded schools in India, here and in America. The questioner says: are you not contradicting yourself when the teachers and the students in all these schools are trying to understand their own conditioning, educating themselves not only academically, but also educating themselves to understand their whole conditioning, their whole nature, their whole psyche? One doesn't quite see the contradiction.

Since the times of ancient Greece and ancient India,

schools have been places where you learn. Learn where there is leisure. Please go with me a little bit. You cannot learn if you have no leisure – that is, time to yourself, time to listen to others, time to inquire. Such a place is a school. The modern schools all over the world are merely cultivating one part of the brain, which is engaged in the acquisition of knowledge, technology, science, biology, theology and the like. They are only concerned with the cultivation of a particular part of the brain which acquires a great deal of knowledge, outer knowledge. That knowledge can be used skilfully to earn a livelihood, or unskilfully, depending on the person. Such schools have existed for thousands of years.

Here in these schools we are trying something entirely different. We are trying not only to educate academically to 'O' and 'A' levels, but also to cultivate an understanding, an inquiry into the whole psychological structure of human beings. Students come already conditioned, so there begins the difficulty. One has not only to help generally to uncondition but also to inquire much more deeply. This is what these schools with which we are connected are trying to do. They may not succeed or they may. But as it is a difficult task, one must attempt it, not always follow the easiest path. This is a difficult subject to go into, but it doesn't create an élite. What is wrong with an élite? Do you want everybody and everything pulled down to the common denominator? That is one of the troubles with so-called democracy.

So there is no contradiction as far as one can see. Contradiction exists only when you assert something at one time and contradict it at another. But here we are saying that no one can lead you to truth, to illumination, to the right kind of meditation, to right behaviour, no one, because each one of us is responsible for himself, not depending on anybody at all. We are trying in all these schools to cultivate a mind, a brain that is holistic, acquiring knowledge for action in the world, but not neglecting the psychological nature of man, because that is far more important than the academic career. To have the capacity to earn a livelihood in the present world, the present civilization, whatever that civilization is, a certain kind of education is apparently necessary, and most schools in the West and in the East are neglecting the other side, which is far deeper and greater. But here we are trying to do both, which is something not done in other schools. We may succeed, we hope we do, but also we may not. That is what we are trying to do. There is no contradiction.

*From* BULLETIN 46, 1984

## Standing against Society

### MADRAS, INDIA, 1981

*Questioner: During your first talk you spoke of standing up against the corrupt and immoral society like a rock protruding from mid-stream in a river. I find this confusing because the rock means to me to be an outsider, and such an outsider in his own life does not need to stand up against anything or anybody. Your clarification and answer are very important to me.*

KRISHNAMURTI: First of all, are we clear at what level, at what depth we are using the word 'corruption'? What does it imply? There is physical corruption – the pollution of the air in the cities, the towns. Human beings are destroying the seas, they have killed 50 million and more whales, they are killing baby seals. Then there is corruption politically, religiously, and so on. Throughout the world, as you travel around, observe, talk to people, you see corruption

95

everywhere, and more so, unfortunately, in this part of the world – passing money under the table; if you want to buy a ticket you have to bribe. The word 'corrupt' means to break up. But basically the corruption everywhere is of the brain and the heart. So we must be clear whether we are talking about financial, bureaucratic and political corruption, or about the corruption of the religious world, which is riddled with all kinds of superstition – just a lot of words that have lost all meaning, repetition of rituals and all that. Is that not corruption? Are not ideals a form of corruption? You may have ideals, say, of non-violence. Because you are violent, you have ideals of non-violence, but while you are pursuing the ideals, you are violent. So is that not corruption of a brain that disregards the action to end violence? And is it not corruption when there is no love at all, only pleasure, which is suffering? Throughout the world this word 'love' is heavily loaded and has been associated with pleasure, with anxiety, with jealousy, with attachment, and is that not corruption? Is not attachment itself corruption? When one is attached to an ideal or to a house or to a person, the consequences are obvious – jealousy, anxiety, possessiveness – all that and more. When you investigate attachment, is it not corruption?

In regard to your question about the simile of standing out like a rock in mid-stream, don't carry the simile too far. A simile is a description of what is taking place, but if you make the simile important, then you lose the significance of what is actually going on.

The society in which we live is essentially based on relationship with each other. If in that relationship there is no love, just mutual exploitation, mutual comfort in various other ways, it must inevitably bring about corruption. So what will you do about all this? This is a marvellous world – the beauty of the world, the beauty of the earth, the extraordinary quality of a tree – and we are destroying the earth as we are destroying ourselves. So how will you as a human being, living here, act? Will we, each one of us, see that we are not corrupt? If our relationship with each other is destructive, constant battle, struggle, pain, despair, then we will inevitably create an environment which will represent what we are. So what are we going to do about it, each one of us? Is this corruption, this lack of integrity, an abstraction, an idea, or is it an actuality which we want to change? It is up to you.

*Questioner: Is there such a thing as transformation? What is it to be transformed?*

KRISHNAMURTI: When you are observing, seeing the dirt on the road, seeing how the politicians behave, seeing your own attitude towards your wife, your children and so on, transformation is there. Do you understand? To bring about some kind of order in daily life, that is transformation; not something extraordinary, out of this world. When one is not thinking clearly, objectively, rationally, be aware of that and change it, break it. That is transformation. If you are jealous watch it, don't give it time to flower, change it immediately. That is transformation. When you are greedy, violent, ambitious, trying to become some kind of holy man, see how it is creating a world of tremendous uselessness. I don't know if you are aware of this. Competition is destroying the world. The world is becoming more and more competitive, more and more aggressive, and if you change it immediately, that is transformation. And if you go very much deeper into the problem, it is clear that thought denies love. Therefore one has to find out whether there is an end to thought, an end to time, not philosophize over it and discuss it, but find out. Truly that is transformation, and if you go into it very deeply, transformation means never a thought of becoming, comparing; it is being absolutely nothing.

*Questioner: I think the saints created idols and stories to teach man how to lead a good and correct life. How can you call it nonsense?*

KRISHNAMURTI: Need the question be answered? First of all who is a saint – the man who struggles to become something? The man who gives up the world? He is not giving up the world, the world is himself. He may be angry and control his anger, but he is boiling inside; he may torture himself, he may be slightly neurotic and you soon begin to worship him. One day in Benares a sannyasi in robes came along, sat under a tree with some kind of stick in his hand and began to shout. Nobody paid any attention to him for four or five days. The speaker was watching all this from his window at Rajghat.* Then an old lady came along and gave him a flower. A few days later there were half a dozen people around him. He has a garland. After a fortnight he becomes a saint. I don't know if you realize this. In the West a man who is slightly deranged is sent to a mental hospital. Here he becomes a saint. I am not being cynical, I am not being rude, insolent, but this is what is happening. A sannyasi is no longer a sannyasi, he is just following a tradition. And have the saints created a different world, a good society, a good human being through their stories, through idols, ideals? You are the result of all this. Are we good human beings, good in the sense of whole, non-fragmented, not broken up – good means also holy? I don't mean good behaviour, being kind, that is only part of it. Being good implies an unbroken, non-fragmented, harmonious human being. Are we that after these thousands of years of saints and Upanishads and Gitas? Or are we just like everybody else? We are humanity. To be good is not to follow. To be good is to be able to understand the whole movement of life.

*Questioner: You say that if one individual changes he can transform the world. May I submit that in spite of your sincerity, love and truthful statements, and that power which cannot be described, the*

---

*Near Benares.

*world has gone from bad to worse? Is there such a thing as destiny?*

KRISHNAMURTI: What is the world? What is the individual? What have individuals done in the world which has influenced the world? Hitler has influenced the world, Mao Tsetung has influenced the world, Stalin has influenced the world, Lenin has, and all the warmongers. That seems obvious. History is full of wars. History over the past 5,000 years records war going on in one part of the world or another year by year. That has affected millions of people. And also the good has influenced the world. You have the Buddha on one side; he has also affected the human mind, human brain, throughout the East. So when we talk about individual change and ask whether that individual change will bring about any transformation in society, I think that is a wrong question to put. Are we really actually concerned about the transformation of society – society which is corrupt, which is immoral, which is based on competition, ruthlessness? That is the society in which we are living. Are you really, deeply interested in changing that, even as a single human being? If you are, then you have to inquire into what is society. Is society a word, an abstraction or a reality? Is it reality or is it an abstraction of human relationship? It is human relationship that is society. That human relationship with all its complexities, its conditions, with its hates, can you alter all that relationship? You can. You can stop being cruel and all that goes with it. What your relationship is, your environment is. If your relationship is possessive and self-centred, you are creating a thing around you which will be equally destructive. So the individual is you and you are the rest of mankind. I don't know if you realize it.

*Questioner: You often switch over from mind to brain. Is there any difference between them? If so, what is the mind?*

KRISHNAMURTI: I am afraid it is a slip of the tongue. I am

only talking about the brain. The questioner wants to know
what is the mind. Is the mind different from the brain? Is
the mind something untouched by the brain? Is the mind
not the result of time? First of all, to understand what the
mind is, we must be very clear how our brain operates –
not according to the brain specialists, not according to the
neurologists, not according to those who have studied a
great deal about the brains of rats and pigeons and all that;
we are studying, each one of us, the nature of our own
brain – how we think, what we think, how we act, what is
our behaviour, what are our immediate spontaneous responses. Are we aware of that? Are we aware that our
thinking is extraordinarily confined within a narrow groove,
that our thinking is mechanical along certain particular
trends of activity, that our education is conditioned by study
towards some career? The scientists now say that thought is
the essence of the brain, which is experience, knowledge,
memory, action. They are actually coming to that! We
have been saying endlessly that thought is a material process. There is nothing sacred about thought, and whatever
thought creates, whether mechanically, idealistically, or in
projecting a future in the hope of reaching some kind of
happiness, peace, it is all the movement of thought. Are we
aware of this, that when you go to a temple, it is nothing
but a material process? You might not like to hear that, but
it is a fact. The architecture of the temple, the mosque, the
church, and all that is put inside the buildings are the result
of thought. Are we really aware of it and therefore moving
in a totally different direction?

When you accept tradition, it makes the mind exceed-
ingly dull, stupid, though you may read the Gita endlessly.
You hold to tradition – that is what is happening both in
the West and in the East. Can you stop all this in yourself,
or are you too dull, so used to the confusion, the misery? So
we have to understand very clearly the activity of the brain,
which is the action of our consciousness, which is the activity

of our psychological world in which we live. The whole of that – the brain, the consciousness, the psychological world, all are one. Would you question that? Probably you have not even thought of it. It is very important to understand what the mind is, to understand what the activities of thought are, which have created the contents of our consciousness and the psychological world in which we live. It is part of thought – the structure which thought has built in man, the 'me' and the 'not me', 'we' and 'they', the quarrels, the battles between each human being. And the brain has evolved through time, evolved through millions of years, accumulating knowledge, experience, memory and so on. It is the result of time. There is no question of argument about it. And is love, compassion with its intelligence, the result, the movement of thought? You understand my question, sir? Can you cultivate love?

*Questioner: I am a student of chartered accountancy. Even though I understand each and every word of J.K., the message remains vague. What should I do to understand his message fully?*

KRISHNAMURTI: Don't understand his message! He is not bringing a message. He is pointing out your life, not his life, not his message. He is pointing out how you live, what is your daily life and one is unwilling to face that. We are unwilling to go into our sorrows, our tortures, anxiety, loneliness, the depressions we go through, the desire to fulfil, to become something. We are unwilling to face all that and want to be led by somebody, including the speaker, wanting to understand the message of the Gita or some other non-sensical book. The speaker says over and over again that he acts as a mirror in which you can see the activity of your own self. And to look very carefully you have to pay attention. You have to listen if you are interested, listen and find out the art of listening, the art of seeing, the art of learning. It is all there as a book which is yourself. The book of mankind is you. Please sir, see the truth of all this. You are unwilling to read that book. You want somebody to tell you about the book or help you to analyse the book, to understand the book. So you invent a priest, a guru, a yogi, the sannyasi who will tell you all about it, and so escape from yourself. Can you read the book which is so ancient, which contains all the history of mankind which is you? Can you read that book carefully, word by word, not distorting it, not listening to one chapter and neglecting the other chapters, not taking one sentence and meditating on it, but the whole book? Either you read the whole book, chapter by chapter, page after page, which will take a long time, your whole life, or is there a way of reading it completely with one glance? Do you understand my question? How can one read this book which is the 'me', which is the 'you', which is mankind with all the experience of misery, suffering, confusion, lack of integrity and all that? How can you read it at one glance, not take month after month? The book is you and if you take time over the book, time is going to destroy the book, the very time is going to destroy because our brain functions in time. So one must have the capacity to listen to what the book, the entire book says, to see clearly, which means that the brain is so alert, so tremendously active that it is the total activity of the brain. Can you observe yourself in the mirror, in the book, that book which is yourself, completely, instantly? Then you will see that the book is nothing. I wonder if you understand? You may read the book from the first page to the last page and you may find that there is nothing in it. Do you understand what I am saying? That means, be nothing, don't become. The book is the becoming, the history of becoming. So if you examine yourself, if you look into yourself, what are you? A physical appearance, short, tall, beard or no beard, man or woman and all the educated capacity, the trivial pursuit. It is all a movement in becoming something, is it not? Becoming what – a business manager getting more money, becoming a saint? When a man tries to become a saint, he is no longer a saint, he is just caught in the track of tradition. So you can glance at the book and see it is absolutely nothing, and live in this world being nothing. Do you understand, sir? No you don't. So, sirs and ladies, you hear all this and perhaps if you are going to travel with the speaker, you will hear it at every talk put in different words, different contexts, different sentences, but to bring about a complete understanding in oneself is far more important than anything else in life, because we are destroying the world; we have no love, no care. So, the speaker has no message; the message is you. The speaker is just pointing out.

*From* BULLETIN 42, 1982

## How to Meet Life

BROCKWOOD PARK, ENGLAND, 3 SEPTEMBER 1981

*Questioner: We find ourselves living in fear of war, of losing a job, if we have one, in fear of terrorism, of the violence of our children, of being at the very mercy of inept politicians. How do we meet life as it is today?*

KRISHNAMURTI: How do you meet it? One must take it for granted that the world is becoming more and more violent – it is obvious. The threats of war are also very obvious, and also the very strange phenomenon that our children are becoming violent. One remembers a mother coming to see us in India some time ago. In the Indian tradition mothers are held in very great respect, and this mother was horrified because, she said, her children had beaten her – an unheard of thing in India. So this violence is spreading all over the

103

world. And there is this fear of losing a job, as the questioner says. Facing all this, knowing all this, how does one meet life as it is today?

I don't know. I know how to meet it for myself, but one doesn't know how you will meet it. First, what is life, what is this thing called existence, full of sorrow, over-population, inept politicians, all the trickery, dishonesty, bribery that is going on in the world? How does one meet it? Surely, one must first inquire what does it mean to live? What does it mean to live in this world as it is? How do we live our daily life, actually, not theoretically, not philosophically or idealistically, but actually how do we live our daily life? If we examine it or are aware of it seriously, it is a constant battle, constant struggle, effort after effort. Having to get up in the morning is an effort. What shall we do? We cannot possibly escape from it. One used to know several people who said that the world was impossible to live in, and they withdrew totally to some Himalayan mountains and disappeared. That is merely an avoidance, an escape from reality, as it is to lose oneself in a commune, or join some guru with vast estates and get lost in that. Obviously, those people do not solve the problems of daily life nor inquire into the change, the psychological revolution of a society. They escape from all this. And we, if we do not escape and are actually living in this world as it is, what shall we do? Can we change our life? To have no conflict at all in our life, because conflict is part of violence – is that possible? This constant struggle to be something is the basis of our life, the struggle to struggle. Can we, as human beings, living in this world, change ourselves? That is really the question – radically, psychologically transform ourselves, not eventually, not admitting time. For a serious man, a really religious man, there is no tomorrow. This is rather a hard saying, that there is no tomorrow; there is only the rich worship of today. Can we live this life wholly, and actually, daily, transform our relationship with each other? That is the real issue, not what the world is, for the world is us. Please see this: the world is you and you are the world. This is an obvious, terrible fact, a challenge that must be met completely – that is, to realize that we are the world with all its ugliness, that we have contributed to all this, that we are responsible for all this, all that is happening in the Middle East, in Africa and all the craziness that is going on in this world, we are responsible for it. We may not be responsible for the deeds of our grandfathers and great-grandfathers – slavery, thousands of wars, the brutality of empires – but we are part of it. If we don't feel our responsibility, which means being utterly responsible for ourselves, for what we do, what we think, how we behave, then it becomes rather hopeless, knowing what the world is, knowing that we cannot individually, separately, solve this problem of terrorism. That is the problem of governments, to see that its citizens are safe, protected, but they don't seem to care. If each government were really concerned to protect its own people, there would be no wars. But apparently governments have lost sanity too, they are only concerned with party politics, with their own power, position, prestige – you know all this, the whole game.

So can we, not admitting time, that is, tomorrow, the future, live in such a way that today is all-important? That means we have to become extraordinarily alert to our reactions, to our confusion – work like fury on ourselves. That is the only thing we can do apparently. And if we don't do that there is really no future for man. I do not know if you have followed some of the headlines in the newspapers – all this preparing for war. And if you are preparing for something, you are going to have it – like preparing a good dish. The ordinary people in the world apparently don't seem to care. Those who are intellectually, scientifically, involved in the production of armaments, don't care. They are only interested in their careers, in their jobs, in their research; and those of us who are fairly ordinary people, so-called middle class, if we don't care at all, then we are really throwing in the sponge. The tragedy is that we don't seem to care. We don't get together, think together, work together. We are only too willing to join institutions, organizations, hoping they will stop wars, stop us butchering each other. They have never done it. Institutions, organizations will never stop any of this. It is the human heart, the human mind that is involved in this. Please, we are not talking rhetorically; we are facing something really very dangerous. We have met some of the prominent people who are involved in all this, and they don't care. But if we care and our daily life is lived rightly, if each one of us is aware of what we are doing daily, then I think there is some hope for the future.

*From* BULLETIN 46, 1984

## The Demands of Society

SAANEN, SWITZERLAND, JULY 1984

*Questioner: How can one reconcile the demands of society with a life of total freedom?*

KRISHNAMURTI: What are the demands of society? Tell me, please. That you go to the office from nine to five, or the factory, that you go to a nightclub for excitement after all the boredom of the day's work, take a fortnight or three weeks' holiday in sunny Spain or Italy? What are the demands of society? That you must earn a livelihood, that you must live in that particular part of the country all your life, practise as a lawyer, or a doctor, or in the factory as a union leader, and so on. Right? Therefore one must also ask the question: what is this society that demands so much, and who created the wretched thing? Who is responsible for this? The church, the temple, the mosque, and all the circus that goes on inside them? Who is responsible for all this? Is the society different from us, or have we created the society, each one of us, through our ambition, through our greed, our envy, our violence, through our corruption, through our fear, wanting our security in the community, in the nation – you follow? We have created this society and then blame the society for what it demands. Therefore you ask: can I live in absolute freedom, or rather, can I reconcile with society and myself seek freedom? It is such an absurd question. Sorry, I am not being rude to the questioner. It is absurd because you *are* society. Do we really see that, not as an idea, not as a concept, or something you must accept? But we, each one of us on this earth for the last 40,000 years or more, have created the society in which we live: the stupidity of religions, the stupidity of the nations arming themselves. For God's sake, we have created it because we insist on being American or French or Russian. We insist on calling ourselves Catholic, Protestant, Hindu, Buddhist, Muslim, and this gives us a sense of security. But it is these very divisions that obstruct the search for security. It is so clear.

So there is no reconciliation between society and its demands and your demands for freedom. The demands come from your own violence, from your own ugly, limited selfishness. It is one of the most complex things to find out for oneself where selfishness is, where the ego very, very subtly hides itself. It can hide politically 'doing good for the country'. It can hide in the religious world most beautifully: 'I believe in God, I serve God', or in social help – not that I am against social help, don't jump to that conclusion – but it can hide there. It requires a very attentive, not analytical, but an observing brain to see where the subtleties of the self, of selfishness, are hidden. Then when there is no self, society doesn't exist; you don't have to reconcile with it. It is only the inattentive, the unaware who say, 'How am I to respond to society when I am working for freedom?' You understand?

If I may point out, we need to be re-educated, not through school, college, university – which also condition the brain – nor through work in the office or the factory. We need to re-educate ourselves by being aware, seeing how we are caught in words. Can we do this? If we cannot do it we are going to have perpetual wars, perpetual weeping, always in conflict, misery and all that is entailed. The speaker is not pessimistic or optimistic; these are the facts. When you live with facts as they are, not with data produced by the computer, but observing them, watching your own activity, your own egotistic pursuits, then out of that grows marvellous freedom with all its great beauty and strength.

*From* BULLETIN 48, 1985

**PART III**

*Talks*

# What is a Religious Mind?

I think we should consider this morning what is a religious mind. I would like to go into it fairly deeply because I feel that only such a mind can resolve all our problems, not only the political and economic problems, but the much more fundamental problems of human existence. Before we go into it, I think we should repeat what we have already said, that a serious mind is a mind that is willing to go to the very root of things and discover what is true and what is false. There is a mind that does not stop halfway and does not allow itself to be distracted by any other consideration. I hope that there are at least a few who are capable of doing this and earnest enough to do it.

I think we are all familiar with the present world situation and do not need to be told of the deceptions, the corruption, the social and economic inequalities, the menace of wars, the constant threats. To understand all this confusion and bring about clarity, it seems to me that there must be a radical change in the mind itself and not just patchwork reform or a mere adjustment. To wade through all this confusion, which is not only outside us but within us, to grapple with all the mounting tensions and the increasing demands, one needs a radical revolution in the psyche itself, one needs to have an entirely different mind.

For me, revolution is synonymous with religion. I do not mean by the word 'revolution' immediate economic or social change; I mean a revolution in consciousness itself. All other forms of revolution, whether Communist, Capitalist or what you will, are merely reactionary. A revolution in the mind, which means the complete destruction of what has been, so that the mind is capable of seeing what is true without distortion, without illusion – that is the way of religion. I think the real, the true religious mind does exist, can exist.

I think, if one has gone into it very deeply, one can discover such a mind for oneself. A mind that has broken down, destroyed, all the barriers, all the lies which society, religion, dogma, belief have imposed upon it, and gone beyond to discover what is true, is the true religious mind.

So, first let us go into the question of experience. Our brains are the result of the experience of centuries. The brain is the storehouse of memory. Without that memory, without the accumulated experience and knowledge, we should not be able to function at all as human beings. Experience – memory – is obviously necessary at a certain level, but I think it is also fairly obvious that all experience based on the conditioning of knowledge, of memory, is bound to be limited. And, therefore, experience is not a factor in liberation. I do not know if you have thought about this at all.

Every experience is conditioned by the past experience. So there is no new experience, it is always coloured by the past. In the very process of experiencing, there is the distortion which comes into being from the past, the past being knowledge, memory, the various accumulated experiences, not only of the individual, but also of the race, the community. Now, is it possible to deny all that experience?

I do not know if you have gone into the question of denial, what it means to deny something. It means the capacity to deny the authority of knowledge, to deny the authority of experience, to deny the authority of memory, to deny the priests, the church, everything that has been imposed on the psyche. There are only two means of denial for most of us – either through knowledge or through reaction. You deny the authority of the priest, the church, the written word, the book, either because you have studied, inquired, accumulated other knowledge, or because you do not like it, you react against it. Whereas true denial implies, does it not, that you deny without knowing what is going to happen, without any future hope? To say, 'I do not know what is true, but this is false,' is, surely, the only true denial, because that denial is not out of calculated knowledge, not out of reaction. After all, if you know what your denial is leading to, then it is merely an exchange, a thing of the market-place and, therefore, it is not true denial at all.

I think one has to understand this a little, to go into it rather deeply, because I want to find out, through denial, what is the religious mind. I feel that through negation one can find out what is true. You cannot find out what is true by assertion. You must sweep the slate completely clean of the known before you can find out.

So, we are going to inquire into what the religious mind is through denial – that is, through negation, through negative thinking. And obviously there is no negative inquiry if denial is based on knowledge, on reaction. I hope this is fairly clear. If I deny the authority of the priest, of the book, or of tradition, because I do not like it, that is just a reaction because I then substitute something else for what I have denied. And if I deny because I have sufficient knowledge, facts, information and so on, then my knowledge becomes my refuge. But there is a denial which is not the outcome of reaction or knowledge, but which comes from observation, from seeing a thing as it is, the fact of it. That is true denial because it leaves the mind cleansed of all assumptions, all illusions, authorities, desires.

So is it possible to deny authority? I don't mean the authority of the policeman, the law of the country and all that; that is silly and immature and will end us up in jail. I mean the denying of the authority imposed by society on the psyche, on the consciousness, deep down; to deny the authority of all experience, all knowledge, so that the mind is in a state of not knowing what will be, but only knowing what is not true.

You know, if you have gone into it so far, it gives you an astonishing sense of integration, of not being torn between conflicting, contradictory desires; seeing what is true, what is false, or seeing the true in the false, gives you a sense of real perception, a clarity. The mind is then in a position – having destroyed all the securities, the fears, the ambitions, vanities, visions, purposes, everything – in a state that is completely alone, uninfluenced.

Surely, to find reality, to find 'God', or whatever name you like to give it, the mind must be alone, uninfluenced, because then such a mind is a pure mind; and a pure mind can proceed. When there is the complete destruction of all things which it has created within itself as security, as hope and as the resistance against hope, which is despair, and so on, then there comes, surely, a fearless state in which there is no death. A mind that is alone is completely living, and in that living there is a dying every minute; and, therefore, for that mind there is no death. It is really extraordinary. If you have gone into that thing you discover for yourself that there is no such thing as death. There is only that state of pure austerity of the mind which is alone.

This aloneness is not isolation; it is not escape into some ivory tower; it is not loneliness. All that has been left behind, forgotten, dissipated and destroyed. So such a mind knows what destruction is; and we must know destruction, otherwise we cannot find anything new. And how frightened we are to destroy everything we have accumulated.

There is a Sanskrit saying: 'Ideas are the children of barren women.' I think most of us indulge in ideas. You may be treating the talks we have been having as an exchange of ideas, as a process of accepting new ideas and discarding old ones, or as a process of denying new ideas and holding on to the old. We are not dealing with ideas at all. We are dealing with fact. And when one is concerned with fact, there is no adjustment; you either accept it or you deny it. You can say, 'I do not like those ideas, I prefer the old ones, I am going to live in my own stew'; or you can go along with the fact. You cannot compromise, you cannot adjust. Destruction is not adjustment. To adjust, to say, 'I must be less ambitious, not so envious,' is not destruction. And one must, surely, see the truth that ambition, envy, are ugly, stupid, and one must destroy all these absurdities. Love never adjusts. It is only desire, fear, hope, that adjust. That is why love is a destructive thing, because it refuses to adapt itself or conform to a pattern.

So we begin to discover that when there is the destruction of all the authority which man has created for himself in his desire to be secure inwardly, then there is creation. Destruction is creation.

Then, if you have abandoned ideas and are not adjusting yourself to your own pattern of existence or a new pattern which you think the speaker is creating, if you have gone that far, you will find that the brain can and must function only with regard to outward things, respond only to outward demands. Therefore, the brain becomes completely quiet. This means that the authority of its experiences has come to an end and, therefore, it is incapable of creating illusions. To find out what is true it is essential for the power to create illusion in any form to come to an end. The power to create illusions is the power of desire, the power of ambition, of wanting to be this and not wanting to be that.

So the brain must function in this world with reason, with sanity, with clarity, but inwardly it must be completely quiet.

We are told by the biologists that it has taken millions of years for the brain to develop to its present stage and that it will take millions of years to develop further. Now, the religious mind does not depend on time for its development. What I want to convey is that when the brain, which must function in its responses to the outward existence, becomes quiet inwardly, then there is no longer the machinery of accumulating experience and knowledge. Therefore, nwardly it is completely quiet, but fully alive, and then it can jump the million years.

So, for the religious mind, there is no time. Time exists only in that state of a continuity moving to a further continuity and achievement. When the religious mind has destroyed the authority of the past, the traditions, the values imposed upon it, then it is capable of being without time. Then it is completely developed. Because, after all, when you have denied time, you have denied all development through time and space. Please, this is not an idea, it is not a thing to be played with. If you have gone through it, you know what it is, you are in that state, but if you have not gone through it, then you cannot just pick up these as ideas and play with them.

So, you find destruction is creation and in creating there is no time. Creation is that state when the brain, having destroyed all the past, is completely quiet and, therefore, in that state in which there is no time or space in which to grow, to express, to become. And that state of creation is not the creation of the few gifted people – the painters, musicians, writers, architects. It is only the religious mind that can be in a state of creation, and the religious mind is not the mind that belongs to some church, some belief, some dogma; these only condition the mind. Going to church every morning and worshipping this or that does not make you a religious person, though respectable society may accept you as such. What makes a person religious is the total destruction of the known.

In this creation there is a sense of beauty, a beauty which is not put together by man, a beauty which is beyond thought and feeling. After all, thought and feeling are merely reactions and beauty is not a reaction. A religious mind has that beauty, which is not the mere appreciation of nature, the lovely mountains and the roaring stream – but quite a different sense of beauty; and with it goes love. I do not think you can separate beauty and love. You know, for most of us love is a painful thing because with it always come jealousy, hate and possessive instincts. But this love of which we are talking is a state of the flame without the smoke.

So, the religious mind knows this complete, total destruction and what it means to be in a state of creation – which is not communicable – and with it there is the sense of beauty and love – which are indivisible. Love is not divisible as divine love and physical love. It is love. And with it goes, naturally, without saying, a sense of passion. One cannot go very far without passion – passion being intensity. It is not the intensity of wanting to alter something, wanting to do something, the intensity which has a cause so that when you remove the cause, the intensity disappears. It is not a state of enthusiasm. Beauty can only be when there is a passion which is austere. The religious mind, being in this state, has a peculiar quality of strength.

You know, for us, strength is the result of will, of many desires woven into the rope of will. And that will is a resistance with most of us. The process of resisting something or pursuing a result develops will and that will is generally called strength. But the strength of which we are talking has nothing to do with will. It is a strength without a cause. It cannot be utilized, but without it nothing can exist.

So, if one has gone so deeply in discovering for oneself, then the religious mind does exist; and it does not belong to any individual. It is the mind; it is the religious mind apart from all human endeavours, demands, individual urges, compulsions, and all the rest of it. We have only been describing the totality of the mind, which may appear divided by the use of the different words, but it is a total thing in which all this is contained. Therefore, such a religious mind can receive that which is not measurable by the brain. That thing is unnameable; no temple, no priest, no church, no dogma can hold it. To deny all that and live in this state is the true religious mind.

*From* BULLETIN 52, 1987

# The Problems of Youth

I don't think the problems of youth, middle age and old age can be separated; youth has not a special problem. It may appear that way because the young are just beginning their lives. Either we make a mess of our lives right from the start, and so are caught in a morass of problems, uncertainties, dissatisfactions and despair, or when we are young – and I think that perhaps is the only time – we lay a right foundation. I do not mean that the older people cannot completely break out of the trap in which they are caught, but it seems much easier for the young to begin to understand what an extraordinary thing life is. Life isn't just sex, smoking pot, taking LSD, going to church or making a name for oneself in business; or throwing up the whole thing in despair and leading a riotous, Bohemian, uncertain kind of existence. I think there is something more important in life, a much deeper issue, which requires a great deal of seriousness. And it is only when one is young that one can sow the seeds of seriousness which will flower and blossom as one lives. But to sow these seeds of clarity, seriousness and right behaviour, one needs careful observation, careful watchfulness.

When one is young one must be *revolutionary*, not merely in revolt; that's fairly easy, that's what everybody does. But to be really revolutionary, in the right sense of the word, not in the Chinese or Communist sense, but to be *psychologically* revolutionary, means non-acceptance of any pattern set by oneself or another, no sense of conformity nor accepting any sort of authority, which means freedom from fear. And out of that freedom one can live a totally different kind of life; not a life established by the older generation with their wars, their comparative living, their gods, their religions, their saviours and priests. All that is dead and finished.

So, it seems to me, that when one is young, when one is uncommitted to a family, a job and all the activities and miseries, it is then that one can begin to sow a seed that will blossom right throughout one's life, instead of getting lost in all the meaningless and absurd pursuits of our daily existence. And that really means a continuous action, which can take place only when there is intensity, urgency and passion; not the superficial urgency of some sexual satisfaction, nor the urgency to conform to a particular pattern of smoking marijuana or taking drugs. These various forms of abuse and indulgence distort the mind and, as one gets older, these distortions become worse. That's why one should not only be aware of outward things, but also of the deep inward movement of desires, pursuits, motives, fears and anxieties.

It's like ploughing a field and then sowing; unfortunately most of us are everlastingly ploughing and digging, but we never seem to sow. The sowing is action, but if that action is the outcome of a particular pattern, then it is not only incomplete, but it breeds all kinds of problems and anxieties. I do not know if you have ever noticed that when you do something *completely*, not only with the intellect but with all your heart and mind, then such an action – which is a complete action – has neither past nor future. It is complete; and in that complete action there is beauty and there is love. And that is what's missing in our lives; we don't know this complete action which has neither the past nor the shadow of the future. It is action which is complete, immediate and urgent. And in that action there is a flame; it may bring about a tremendous revolution outwardly as well as inwardly. You have noticed how a river changes course when it is blocked by a big rock; the whole river has taken a totally different turn. In the same way an action which is whole, which is complete, not touched by our environment, by our inclination or personal tendencies, such an action does bring about a different way of life. And, after all, that's what we are concerned with in these discussions, the actual daily living, also the dialogue one has with oneself tomorrow or next month. In that living there is so little beauty, there is never a complete action and, therefore, no sense of that perfume which one may call love. Most of us are self-centred; all our activities are hedged about by this craving which is the very centre of our existence, which is the 'me'.

I feel it is important to learn to be very simple with ourselves – and that is one of the most difficult things to be. We are never *simple*. Our mind is so complex, our intellect so cultivated and sophisticated; it has innumerable reasons for doing and not doing. The simplicity of which we are speaking is not living any old way in dirt and squalor with few clothes, but the simplicity of direct perception – to see something clearly – and the seeing is the acting. This does bring about an extraordinary simplicity of action. When you do something without a great deal of mentation, but because you can see very clearly without any distortion, then it is there, actually 'what is'. And this very seeing and doing bring about an extraordinary sense of freedom. Without this freedom – not as an idea, but actually to be free inwardly – I don't quite see how life, with its vast complex of problems, demands, activities and pursuits, can possibly be understood. But unfortunately most of us don't want to be free; freedom is a danger, something to be avoided, or when it is there, to be controlled, put in a cage. And the mind does that remarkably well, to trap freedom and to hold it.

We have so many questions. What am I to do living in this world, which is violent, insane, brutal and cruel? What is my relationship with the rest of the world? How am I to act in that relationship? All these are very serious problems. Most of us try to bring about some peripheral activity; we want to reform or correct the world. We say, 'I see very clearly the necessity of not being violent, so somehow I must affect the world.' I think one does tremendously affect the world if, in oneself, one is not violent, not as an idea, but actually. To live every day at peace within oneself, a life which is not competitive, not ambitious or envious, a life which does not create enmity. Then, living in this world, I have a relationship with it.

You see, *what I am* matters enormously, because I have created this society; I have put it together with my demands, my prejudices, my hatreds, my religions and my nationalism. I have divided the world into fragments and if I, in myself, am divided, my relationship with the world will be broken; it will have very little meaning. But if I do not function in fragments, but act completely, totally, then I have quite a different relationship with the world. But we want to be told what that relationship will be through words, through images, through symbols; we want the pattern of this relationship of an individual who is free, whose action is complete. But the word, the symbol, is not the fact; nevertheless we are satisfied with words and explanations. But if we, as human beings, could effect within ourselves a non-fragmentary world, then I think all relationship would undergo a tremendous revolution. And, after all, any movement that is worthwhile, any action that has deep significance must begin within ourselves, within each one of us. I first must change. I must see what is implied in the nature, the structure of that relationship with the world; and the very seeing of it is the doing. And therefore, as a human being living in this world, I bring about a different quality altogether, and that quality, it seems to me, is a religious mind.

I do not know if you have *felt* deeply what that word 'religious' implies. Surely it is not the religion of organized belief and propaganda, of the churches, the priests, the ceremonies and the rituals. That is not religion. I feel religion is something entirely different. It has nothing whatever to do with what man has invented through fear. This so-called religion is something which man has sought and caught in the trap of organized religions. We are talking of the religious mind, which is extraordinarily difficult to explain because so many things are involved. Surely a religious mind implies a state of mind in which there is no fear at all, and therefore no sense of security at any time; in such a mind there is no belief whatsoever, only *what is*, what actually is. And in that mind there is a state of silence which is not produced by thought, but which is the natural outcome of a great deal of awareness and attention. It is the result of meditation in which the meditator is totally absent; then out of that comes a silence in which there is neither the observer nor the observed. And in that silence one begins to discover for oneself the origin and beginning of thought. One then realizes that thought is always old and that therefore it can never discover anything new. And finding all this out of that silence – which is part of the religious mind – one knows a state of energy which is not the energy of conflict, nor is it the energy engendered through striving, ambition, greed and envy. It is an energy untouched by any kind of conflict. All that, it seems to me, is the state of the religious mind.

Without coming upon that, you may take LSD, have innumerable visions or experiences, be in a state of heightened sensitivity, or mesmerize yourself through the repetition of various dogmas and creeds; but these sensations do not contain that quality of the religious mind. So what is important – whether one is very young or very old – is to bring the whole process of one's life to a different level, to a different dimension – now, in the present, at this very moment.

*From* BULLETIN 12, 1971–2

# A Quality of Mind That Knows No Separation

It seems to me that the first thing to understand – in this chaotic and rather mad world – is how to listen to the conclusions, descriptions and analyses that people offer with regard to the problems that we all have. We have so many problems. Not only in this deteriorating country, but also throughout the world, human beings are faced with extraordinarily complex problems. The experts, the intellectuals, the gurus, the theologians, the priests, offer explanations, each according to their particular conditioning, their particular belief and so on. And the more one is confused, the more one is in sorrow, the more one seeks, then the more one wants comfort, security or clarity. There are those who offer security and clarity, and I think it is wise to learn how to listen to what is offered by them (how to listen, not only to them, but also to the speaker), because we are so gullible, we want to accept, we want to be deceived, we want to be hypnotized by words, we want an easy way out of our confusion and sorrow. We are eager – most unfortunately – to accept, especially from those who, according to a formula, explain how to meet the crisis that exists throughout the world; their formulas vary according to their conditioning, according to the culture in which they have been brought up.

Human beings throughout the world have been conditioned according to formulas and concepts for thousands of years and when life – which is a movement – demands your total attention you cannot give it, for you are functioning and thinking according to a formula, whether given by Shankara or Marx or Lenin, or the latest guru that you have. So one has to ask: why is it that human beings through-out the world live by formulas? I do not know if you have ever questioned why you always live at the conceptual level, why you always formulate an ideology and attempt to live and think at that level; *whereas actuality is something entirely different.* Actuality is the daily living which has nothing whatever to do with concepts; that is the first thing to realize. One has to scrap completely all the formulas, all the methods; one has to rethink the whole thing anew; one can no longer be a Hindu, a Christian, a Buddhist, a Muslim. As a human being – living in this country, in this dreadful town with all its miseries, squalor, dirt – one can no longer think in terms of formulas if one is to live a life every minute that is complete, total.

Living is relationship. You cannot be related to another according to a formula – you understand? It is very simple. You have to live, you have to go to your office or factory and labour, strive; but if you try to live according to an image or formula, established by your ancient teachers, you are not related at all – you are merely living according to an idea. It is the same in a Communist state in which they have established an ideology, by tyranny, by conditioning the people – as the Christians have done, as the Hindus have done; they have conditioned the people by words, by propaganda, by incessant repetition.

Your mind functions at an ideological level, at a con-ceptual, abstract level, whereas living is the daily contact, the daily sorrow, misery, loneliness, despair is what we have to understand, not the abstraction, not the brilliant articles written by clever writers. When our daily life is so heavily clothed with ideologies it becomes shoddy, confusing, mean-ingless.

What one has to do is to be aware of one's conditioning – just to know that one is conditioned, that one has been conditioned for centuries. If you do not realize this then you will continue to create great confusion, great misery, for others and for yourself.

We do not know what love is; we do not love, we have become brutal, callous, indifferent, ruthless. Without love you can solve nothing. Have you ever asked yourselves why it is that you have no love at all? You know what I mean by love? – just to be kind without any motive; just to be generous; to feel for others; to feel the ugliness of a filthy street, to feel the poverty; to see this explosion of population going on throughout the world, to feel it, to find out why, to cry, not over your own miserable little family, or a little death of someone whom you like, but to cry for the complete chaos of this world.

All feeling has been lost because we have become so very clever. Cleverness is worldliness – do realize it. When we are clever we are really worldly; we have become clever through education; we have become clever because over-population forces us to struggle hard to live – competing, driving out others by our cleverness, by passing exams and getting a job. We have become clever through the desire for mere survival – watch yourself. We never discuss realities – how to end war, how to be kind, how to be generous – yet we are always willing to discuss abstract things.

I mean by love, a quality of mind that knows no separation – you understand? For when there is separation there is conflict, there is envy, there is jealousy, antagonism, the desire for power, position – the results of our clever worldliness. When there is separation between you and another, there is no relationship – though you may be married, have children, have sex – and when you feel separate from another you have no love, and without love you will not be able to solve the problems of this world or any problem with which you are faced. Do please realize this fundamental issue: you have no love – and why? Why isn't it bubbling in you when you see the beauty of a sunset or a tree, when you see sorrow, misery, confusion, the agonizing existence of man? Why have you no love? That is the fundamental question – not whether God exists or not, not what is going to happen to you when you die; but why haven't you, as human beings, this quality of mind that goes beyond all separation, that goes beyond all nationalities, all religions and their beliefs, their dogmas and all the inventions man has brought about to protect himself. Why? Do ask yourself, please. This is really a very important question – don't brush it off.

Why is it that you, as a human being – so capable, so clever, so cunning, so competitive, having achieved so much technologically, capable of going to the moon or living for weeks under the sea, inventing the extraordinary electronic brain – why is it that you have not the one thing that matters? Without love you become bitter, you are afraid, all relationship is conflict. I do not know if you have ever seriously faced this issue as to why your hearts are empty.

This is not an emotional, sentimental, gathering. *Love is not sentimental, or emotional, it has nothing whatsoever to do with devotion, or loyalty.* One has to find out why one has no love; and in the finding perhaps one will come upon it. One cannot cultivate love, one cannot achieve love through practising a method; there is no school to which you can go and learn. And without love – do what you will, go to all the temples in the world, read all the so-called sacred books – without love your life will be in confusion, your life will be in sorrow.

What your daily life is, your society is. You understand, sirs? Society is not different from you, from what you are, what you have been – that is, the community in which you live. Social disorder exists because you are disorderly in your own life. Yet order cannot come about through intellectual organization, through a plan – we have tried all these things for thousands of years; so many human beings have endeavoured to create a new society, a new community, a new way of living, and they have all failed, and they will always fail, because they build on a formula, on a concept, on an ideology.

So we are going to find out whether we can give our hearts to solve this problem of existence – the daily torture of living, the daily misery, the daily confusion, the passing joy, the passing pleasure which is called life. You cannot solve it without understanding it, which is to love it. You cannot love if you do not know what is involved in separation and what relationship means; we are going to examine that, not intellectually, not verbally, but actually. To do this is to look, to observe what your actual relationship is – the daily relationship with your wife, with your family, with your boss, with your neighbour – and to see whether it is at all possible to go beyond this separative, narrow existence.

First of all, do not be caught by words – you understand? The word is not the actual thing, the word 'tree' is not the actual tree – that's simple. The word will not help you to touch the tree; you have to come into contact with it, to put your hand upon it. We are slaves to words, slaves to ideas, images and symbols. To come into touch with something directly the word must not interfere. So one has to learn the art of *seeing* and *listening*, and to find out how to look; how to look at the world in which you live; how to look at a tree, at a cloud, at the beauty of the sunset. To see something very clearly you must be sensitive – you understand? – and if your hands are hard, brutal, cruel, you cannot touch the tree. If your eyes are blind with your worries, with your gods, with your wife, with your sex, with your fears, you cannot see the cloud, the beauty of the sunset.

One has to learn how to look, how to see, and this art cannot be learnt from another, you have to do it yourself. When the speaker is explaining, do not be carried away by the explanation, but actually do it. Don't say, 'I will try and do it' – that's one of the most evasive statements you can ever make. Either you do it, or you don't do it – there is no trying, or doing your best.

When you look at a leaf, how do you look at it? You obviously look at it with your eyes, but also you look at it with your mind – the mind which has its own memory of that leaf, the botanical name of that leaf. So you look with your eyes, but you also look through associated memories – right? There is a dual process going on. You see with your eyes and also you see through your memory, through the image that you have about that leaf, or about your wife or husband, or about the cloud.

When you look at your husband or wife, you look at him or her with the image that you have built through many years from the memories of sex, of pleasure, of irritation, of nagging, of angry words, and so on; you have built images about each other – that is an actual fact. Now, it is merely these two images that are related, and for this reason you have no direct relationship at all; there is a separation – there must be a separation – hence conflict, and hence the total absence of love. As long as you are not aware of the mechanism, structure and nature of the image, then you will never be free of it and you will always be in conflict.

The world needs co-operation – this country needs it desperately. This country, which is dividing itself so catastrophically through linguistic division, through petty national division, and so on, must have co-operation to live at all. How can you co-operate with another if you have no love? How can you use that word 'co-operation' when you are ambitious, separative, competitive, dividing yourself by words, by beliefs, by dogmas? Yet when you know how to co-operate truly, then you will also know how not to co-operate – you must know both. When you know the meaning and the depth and the significance of co-operation, then you will know the moment for the right action of non-co-operation. But first one must know how to co-operate, and there can be no co-operation if there is separation. Separation will always exist – though you live in a family, though you sleep with your wife or husband – if you have an

image. See first that because of your image of ambition, of
greed, envy and success – though you may live in the same
house, beget children – both of you are separate, you are
not co-operating. Co-operation can only come when there
is love; love is not sentimental, it has nothing to do with
emotionalism; love is not pleasure, love is not desire. To
come upon this extraordinary thing, the beauty of it, you
must learn how to look, to look at the tree, to look at your
wife and children.

Why have human beings come to this extraordinary crisis,
this crisis of total disorganization, this disorder, this confusion within themselves which is expressed outwardly in
society? Why has man, who has lived for so many thousands
and thousands of years, come to such misery and conflict?
Why? This chaos has become so frightening. What is the
reason for it? You will say, 'It is the over-population' –
twelve and a half million people are born every year in
India, which is already over-populated. You will say, 'It is
the morality that goes with technological knowledge.' You
will say, 'It is the lack of communication.' These are the
slick, easy answers. In such an easy answer you won't find
the depth or the truth of the matter. Why is it that you, in
this country, who have lived for so long, with your teachers,
with your Shankaras, Gitas, gurus, with the immature
saints, why is it that you find yourselves now *actually* in this
state, in disorder, in this confusion? Why? If you put aside
the easy explanations of over-population, lack of morality,
which goes with technological knowledge and this lack of
direct communication – which may be true – what then is
the fundamental reason, the fundamental cause of this
misery? Why is it that a country like this, that has had the
tradition of goodness, kindliness, of not killing, not being
brutal – not that you lived it – why, when you have had all
these teachers, why is it and whence is it that something has
gone totally wrong?

To go into it, you must examine very closely; to examine,

you must not be prejudiced; to find out, you must be free and unafraid. We are going to find out – that is, find out the cause; but the finding-out of the cause is not going to help you to be free of the cause – please do understand this. You may know that you feel ill because you have cancer; but knowing that you have cancer does not free you from that disease, you may have to have a surgical operation. Similarly, you may find the cause of your sorrow, but this does not free you from the effect of it; what frees you from the effect of it is the immediate understanding of the cause – the surgical operation on it. You have to look, you have to examine the cause, and for this there must be freedom; you might be frightened, because freedom implies total negation of the past, total negation of your gods, your beliefs, your rituals – total denial of all that. Most people are frightened to be free, yet it is only the free mind – the eager mind, the mind that is awake – that can really find out how this calamity, this immense sorrow has come upon the human being.

So to take the journey the first thing to ensure is that you travel lightly, without all your burdens, without all your prejudices and worries. And that is to bring about a total revolution in ourselves; a total mutation of the mind must take place; and it cannot take place if you are not free to find out, afraid of what may happen.

If you are lucky enough and find out how to listen, how to see, then you will find for yourself that there is a benediction in the very act of seeing, in the very act of listening – not the benediction from a god, there is no benediction from gods, there is no benediction from prayers, or from the temples – a benediction that comes only when you know how to love.

*From* BULLETIN 20, 1973–4

# Love Cannot be Taught

BOMBAY, INDIA, JANUARY 1968

Why do we listen to any speaker? Is it to get some ideas, to learn something? Is it merely out of curiosity? Or do we listen to discover for ourselves, in the words of the speaker, what actually we are? It is a surprising fact that wherever one goes the audience seems to be merely listening to a lot of words, theories and possibilities. And I am afraid that it is the same thing here: as you are sitting there with the speaker on the platform, one wonders at this strange phenomenon; and it is quite strange, because if we knew how to look, how to look at the world with all its multifarious activities, and also knew how to look at ourselves, then I think we would never attend a meeting, we would never listen to another to learn, because in ourselves the whole history of man is written; in ourselves, if we know how to look, how to listen, we can read very clearly the whole story, the misery and the strife of man. We think that somebody else is going to teach us how to look, somebody else is going to show us the way and save us from our endless strife and misery. If you observe, both outwardly and inwardly, you will realize there is no one that can give us the key, the understanding, to our own desperately puzzling, complex, miserable life. But we refuse to look, we refuse to listen to the promptings, to the intimations of that thing which is telling us the story both in detail and in totality, comprehensively – that which is telling us what is actually taking place.

And so, if I may point out, the speaker has nothing to teach you, and he really means it – no new philosophy, no new system or new path to reality. There is no path to reality; the many paths that man has invented to reality are born out of fear; actually there is no path at all. A path implies something that is permanent, static, that is there, immovable; all that you have to do is to tread the path and you will get there. I am afraid it is not a bit like that. It is much more complex, much more subtle and extraordinarily beautiful, if one understands that there is no path, that there is no saviour, that no one can free us from our own confusion, our strife and the endless seeking. Because, as we said, everything is there, if you know how to explore, how to look; it is all in ourselves, for we are the result of time, the result of infinite experience, of vast tradition.

We want to be told how to look, how to listen, what to do. Don't ask those questions, ever, of anybody – what to do, how to listen, how to be aware. All that you have to do is to look. It is not a matter of how to look – just look, with all your heart, with your mind, so that you see things actually as they are. We refuse to look because our hearts are so filled with the things of the mind – the mind, which has so many images that we can look with neither clarity nor affection. And affection cannot be taught; there is no school, there is no teacher, no book, to bring about this quality of love. And without it – do what you will, go to all the temples, to all the mosques, to the churches, sacrifice yourselves, commit yourselves to a particular course of action, belong to a certain political party – but without love, your misery, the confusion, the aching loneliness and despair will never go.

Freedom cannot be given; freedom is something that comes into being when you do not seek it; it comes into being only when you know that you are a prisoner, when you know for yourself *completely* the state of being conditioned, when you know how you are held by society, by culture, by tradition, held by what you have been told. Freedom is order – it is never disorder – and one must have freedom, completely, both outwardly and inwardly; without freedom there is no clarity; without freedom you can't love; without freedom you can't find truth; without freedom you cannot go beyond the limitation of the mind. You must have freedom, and you must demand it with all your being. When you so demand it, you will find out for yourself what order is – and order is not the following of a pattern, a design; it is not the outcome of habit.

Please do listen to all this – just listen, neither accepting nor rejecting.

Without freedom there is only disorder. Disorder, within society, is never morality; this society, as it is, thrives on disorder. Watch it! You can observe each man in competition with the other; each man envious of the other; each man seeking his own security; each man seeking power, position and prestige for himself and for his family. And out of this struggle and conflict man has developed a certain morality, *the morality of adjustment to disorder* – that morality is considered virtue, is considered respectable. But such morality, the morality of society, is not morality at all; it is immorality that has created the pattern of society, its culture, its religions, its education, its government. You can see, if you pay a little attention to it, how each man is frightened, each man is seeking his own security, each man is wanting to fulfil himself (yet never trying to find out if there is such a thing as fulfilment), each man wanting to reach the top of the heap, which is considered success.

We must have freedom to bring about order, for society, as it is, is totally disorderly and, in ourselves we are disorderly. We must bring about order, not the order of government, not the order of the law, of a disintegrating society, but the order which comes when one is aware of and understands this disorder both outwardly and inwardly; without order there is no virtue; there is only that terrible thing called respectability.

To find this absolute order (not that one *finds* it) – as there is order in mathematics, absolute order – one has to come upon it, and that is only possible when one understands the disorder within. We are disorderly, we say one thing, think another, and do something else; we are dishonest to ourselves. This disorder is the search to find psychological security. Obviously one must have outward security, one must have a home, clothes, food – that security is essential; but that outward security is destroyed by the demand for inward, psychological security, the security in belief, the security in ideologies and in relationships. There is no security psychologically; there is no permanency of any kind inwardly; the gods, the beliefs, the ideologies that have been invented, are the product of this search for inward security; and the gods are worshipped so utterly uselessly that they have no meaning at all, they are all the inventions of our petty little minds.

One can see how all this disorder has come into being: when man is ambitious, striving, competing to gain success, he must be ruthless; an ambitious man breeds disorder and he will never know what love is. When you, out of fear, believe one thing, and when another, out of his fear, believes something else – his god and your god, his country and your country, you an Indian, he a Pakistani – that is disorder. So your beliefs, your religions and ideologies, your communities, your families, have created this disorder – do look at it. In this disorder we try to bring about order; we say 'we must' and 'we must not', 'this is right', 'that is wrong' – all within the pattern of disorder. And order, which is virtue, is as clean and absolute as is the order in mathematics. You must have order, otherwise there is no peace, otherwise you will never know what meditation is. Such order is not habit – the repetition of something over and over again. It comes when you have understood disorder, and have totally denied it in yourself; it comes when you are no longer greedy and envious, when you are no longer frightened, when you have completely abandoned your particular little ideology, your gods and your country;

out of that total denial of disorder comes order; through negation comes the positive. For that negation you must have a very highly disciplined mind, a discipline that is not suppression, not control, that is not imitation. To understand disorder, both outwardly and inwardly, to observe, to listen to the discord, to the confusion, *is* discipline, isn't it? To listen to the speaker is discipline; it means that you are giving your attention, it means that you are completely giving your heart and mind – I hope you are. To give your heart and mind is in itself discipline; and there is beauty in that discipline. You have to become a disciple – not to somebody else – a disciple who is learning, learning to see the disorder; in seeing that disorder there is order; you don't have to do a thing, yet you have to work tremendously hard to look.

When you give attention – attention with your heart and mind – that attention is discipline and it is virtue. There is no virtue if you are inattentive; it is inattention that creates disorder.

So, this is the foundation for meditation, one of the most marvellous things.

Do not specially pay attention to the word 'meditation'. I see you are familiar with the word, but the word is not the thing. Suddenly I see in your faces a serious quality creeping in, and at the mention of that word you suddenly sit up more straight. How human beings are slaves to that word! – you don't know what it means. All that you know is that the word denotes some fancy which you have. You know there are those schools and those swamis and yogis going around the world teaching various forms of meditation – don't laugh, you are all doing it in your own way. You think that by repeating certain words you are going to reach the most extraordinary state, by repeating a mantra you will achieve some miraculous experience. That is not meditation at all, it is nonsense, it is self-deception and self-hypnosis. Meditation is something much more vast, more profound. But you cannot come to it by merely playing with 'words' and 'energies'; yet you must come to it, for without it you will never know what love is, you will never have tears in your eyes out of sheer joy, you will never know what beauty is. You may have shoddy little experiences through drugs, through the repetition of words, through the worship of an image, and those experiences, for which human beings crave, are their own self-projections – what they experience is from what has already been known. Please go into it and you will see; you cannot 'experience' something if you do not recognize what it is. If you recognize it, it is already the old. So when you crave for vast experience and are able to recognize it, it is already from memory, a reprojection of that which has been, a remembrance; and this is not meditation.

Meditation is the state of mind which is free; not free *from* anything, but free without any motive – it is not a result. It can only come when there is absolute order, not order according to a pattern or order established through habit or tradition. When there is order there is virtue, the virtue which is not of society, which has nothing whatsoever to do with respectability, with tradition, or with the morality that is developed through disorder.

Virtue is a living thing; it is like a flower, full of beauty, full of perfume, yet it cannot be cultivated. Virtue is a movement, and as with all living things, you cannot capture it, hold it, and say you are virtuous. And without freedom, order, discipline, virtue – which are all the same thing really – meditation is merely so-called, it is a mere escape, an escape from reality, an escape from daily life. But order, freedom and discipline are in daily life; so daily life is meditation – you understand? I hope you understand it. Meditation is in daily life, in the way you smile, the way you look at another, it is in the care, the tenderness, the generosity; it is aware of the anger, the brutality, the violence, the aggression that is – there is the meditative mind.

When you have this total order – not fragmentary order; not order in one part of your mind and the rest in disorder; order is not fragmentary, order is absolute just as two and two make four, they don't make five – there is sanity. There is disorder because we are insane with our beliefs, with our dogmas, with our possessions and attachments; we are insane because at the root of it all there is fear. So, when you have meditatively laid the foundation in daily life – the words you use, the gestures, the feeling, the passion in daily life – then you lay the foundation of order and we can proceed.

You will see that meditation is not concentration. Concentration – which is a narrow, exclusive, separative process – has nothing whatsoever to do with meditation. You see, sirs, to find out the truth you must deny everything that has been said by anybody, deny your guru, your religion, your books. Deny being an Indian, a Muslim, a Christian, an Englishman or a German, deny it completely; then in that denial (and it depends how you deny it, because if you deny out of reaction, then you will create another disorder), you see the truth as truth in disorder, because there is truth in seeing how disorder comes into being – as you see the false in the true.

So then, because freedom – with its order, virtue and discipline – is not fragmentary, there is no longer fragmentation in the structure and the nature of the mind. The mind therefore no longer lives in a state of strife and conflict; such a mind then has no end, it is vast, incredibly deep, it cannot be measured. Such a mind – which in itself has become the immeasurable – lives in affection, with love and with beauty. And when there is beauty and love, there is truth, and no god that the mind of man has invented.

The mind that has understood daily living and has brought order in that daily living, and therefore beauty and love, is a religious mind. Such a mind has no sorrow, such a mind is a benediction, and there is immense, immeasurable bliss.

This constant is love, but the word is not the thing. It has its own movement, its own beauty, which thought – however highly sensitive, subtle – can never capture. Thought must be completely still, and then perhaps the constant can come to touch it. Meditation is perceiving these two as not-duality.

Meditation is seeing the constant touching the ever-changing movement of life. The man who has progressed through being a sinner to being a saint has progressed from one illusion to another. This whole movement is an illusion. When the mind sees this illusion it is no longer creating any illusion, it is no longer measuring. Therefore thought has come to an end with regard to becoming better. Out of this comes a state of liberation – and this is sacred. This alone can, perhaps, receive the constant.

*From* BULLETIN 22, 1974

# The Understanding of Sorrow

BOMBAY, INDIA, FEBRUARY 1968

I do not know if you have asked yourselves seriously whether sorrow can ever end. Man has suffered – not only physically, but inwardly, psychologically – for untold time. He has followed a pattern of endless sorrow, the pattern of living and dying – both offering deep sorrow. Man has not been able, throughout the centuries, to resolve this problem.

Is it at all possible for man – living always in corruption, in a society that is disintegrating – to live life happily, intelligently, which means sensitively, with great inward joy, a joy that has never been touched by sorrow? If one actually asks that question of oneself, I wonder what one could answer. One would probably say that it is not possible, let's forget about it; one would say that one has to live in this ugly world, with pain, old age and death, with the occasional joy which has no motive, or that one is caught in a vicious circle that has no opening.

But without ending sorrow I do not see how one can ever be enlightened, how one can ever have wisdom. Wisdom is not something that you buy in a bookshop, or something that has been accumulated; it is not born of tradition, nor does it come through experience. Wisdom comes only when there is the ending of sorrow; the ending of sorrow *is* wisdom. But we do not know how to end sorrow; we have never given our hearts and minds to find out whether it is at all possible for man to end sorrow, to live a different life, a life that does not produce this aching misery, confusion and fear. We have become very clever in analytical investigation, very intellectual, very smart in giving explanations – like a man who is always ploughing and never, never sowing. This cleverness has made us very worldly; worldliness is this fragmentary cultivation of the mind which has become so astonishingly sharp, so knowing – never saying, 'I don't know.' Worldliness is this lack of humility. Humility is not a thing to be cultivated as you cultivate a tree, a garden or a fragment of the mind. Humility is not of time; for this reason you cannot say, 'I *will* be humble; in time I *will* have that extraordinary, simple state of mind that is always a movement of learning, seeing, listening.'

Wisdom comes with humility. There is humility when you know yourself as you actually are; but when you have a theory, based on the higher self, the lower self, the atman and all the rest of it, invented by the imagination, that is vanity. It is only a mind that is free from the state of sorrow that can love and know the beauty of love; it can see something completely with one glance – the whole beauty of the earth and the sky, the evening star or a flock of birds rising in the morning. It can see all that with one glance and know the quality of beauty, which is love.

Humility is necessary to ask the question: can a mind, which has lived for 10,000 years, ever be in a state where sorrow never touches it? To put that question and to find that quality of mind that is completely innocent, we must understand the whole structure and the nature of experience. Man has had, and is having every day, every minute, thousands and thousands of experiences; he cannot avoid experience, it is there whether he likes it or not, it is impinging on his mind, whether he is conscious or unconscious of it. Can his mind – which is the outcome of time, of tradition, the outcome of man's untold misery – ever be free of experience? Most unfortunately we think that experience is necessary, we think that we must have multitudinous experiences of every kind so as to enrich the mind, so that the mind becomes extraordinarily supple, clear, having passed through so much, read so much, lived so much. We think experience, whether great or small, is an essential part of life; we demand constantly more experience – the experience of sex, of God, of virtue, of family, of travelling – and we endure the daily, monotonous, lonely experience that we have when we are by ourselves. We have accepted this way of living.

With experience comes comparison. I do not know if you have lived without comparing, without comparing yourself with another who is more intelligent, more bright, who has a bigger position, more power and prestige, without comparing yourself with another whose face is more beautiful, who has a brighter smile, a clearer look. Endless comparison goes on within oneself; that is the better, the more; the comparison of what has been with what should be; the measurement that goes on constantly, endlessly, as when you read an advertisement: 'Buy this, it will make you more bright'; 'Use that, it will give you something else'. When there is comparison, you must inevitably invite experience; we think that if we do not compare, if we do not measure, we are dull, we are stupid, and that there is no progress. We compare one picture with another, one writer with another, one fortune with another; we think we reach some understanding of human existence through the comparative study of religions and anthropological investigation. Would we be dull if we did not compare? Or do we only know dullness through comparison – because another is sensitive, has bright eyes, lives without confusion? Is it in comparing yourself with that person that you become aware that your eyes are dull, that the quality of your mind is confused? Does that comparison help you to really understand? Technologically there must be comparison, otherwise scientific knowledge would not exist, but apart from that, why do you compare at all? – and if you did not compare, what would happen?

As you are listening, let your mind watch itself; you will see that it is always caught in comparing and measuring; this brings about dissatisfaction, and, being dissatisfied, you want more. You want to find contentment and therefore invite this endless experience.

What is experience? You must understand what it is before we go further into something that requires a great deal of understanding; we are going to talk about a mind that is totally innocent, for it is only the innocent mind, the very, very simple mind, that can see what is true, that can see clearly. A mind that is full of experience is a complicated mind; every experience has left an imprint on that mind, and such a mind, do what it will, can never know the bliss of innocency.

One has to inquire into the nature of experience; the word means 'to go through', yet the mind never 'goes through' an experience, never 'goes through' it and finishes with it. Every experience leaves a mark, and because there are other marks, other imprints of previous experiences, so every new experience is translated by the previous experience, by the previous imprint, by the previous memory. Do watch it in yourself. One discovers that experience can never set the mind free – *never*; one sees that any experience one recognizes is only recognizable because one has already experienced it – otherwise one cannot recognize it.

Experience leaves an imprint; this is an obvious fact. You have insulted me and my reaction to that insult has left a memory; next time I meet you I meet you with that memory, and by meeting you who have insulted me that memory thickens; or if you have praised me, said, 'What a marvellous chap you are,' again that flattery leaves an imprint, a memory, and next time I meet you there is a thickening of that memory; we become friends. Experience has left imprints, both pleasant and u npleasant. Now can experience be lived, gone through as it occurs, so that when you insult me I receive that insult so completely that it leaves no mark on the mind at all, so that it leaves no memory, or, similarly, when you flatter me, that flattery leaves no mark? – which means the mind is no longer accumulating experience. Please do understand the essence of this. The mind, when the insult or the praise is given to it, is so clear, so sharp, that it meets it totally, because it has rejected experience. Please, do it next time – *do it*, not just try to do it, or do your best to do it, but actually do it because you understand very clearly that experience never sets the mind free.

The religious people want experience; they repeat some word by which a hysteria is produced, which will offer an experience of something beyond; and many of the younger generation take drugs in order to have some sort of 'transcendental' experience. It is always the same problem: man – who has lived a life that is so utterly meaningless, so desperately, inwardly poor, so monotonous, set in such imitative routine – naturally wants something that will give him greater joy, greater vision, greater significance; so he is always looking for experience – which you are doing. You want proof, you want to seek it, find it; that is, you want to experience it. But when you really understand the nature of experience, when you see how it is built, see the truth of it, and, seeing the truth of it, no longer compare, then you no longer follow, then there is no authority; you see that nobody will lead you to greater heights of experience.

If you understand that all measurement invites experience, that the desire for more experience breeds those people who assume authority – the priest, the monk, the man who knows more; if you understand that, you can then inquire into this question of sorrow and of why man suffers, not only physically from grave disease, but also why he suffers when someone dies, why he suffers when he cannot achieve, fulfil, why he feels suddenly lonely when there is no support and there is no one to rely on, when he is left completely alone – why he suffers at all. And, as we said, to understand this there must be humility; but you are not humble, you have read much too much, seeking out the reason why sorrow comes and how it can be ended. So you have become, in seeking the ending of sorrow, very worldly; you have learned how to avoid sorrow – cunningly to avoid it.

To understand sorrow and the ending of sorrow, you have to understand fear; not 'understand' intellectually or verbally, but understand by actually coming to grips with fear so that you are faced with the fact itself. When you are faced with the fact, thought does not operate; when you are faced with a great shock, with a grave crisis, thought does not enter. I do not know if you have noticed that. As soon as thought enters, time is brought into being. (Have I got to explain all this – how thought breeds time, how time is sorrow, how time is fear? Need I explain it? Yes? Too bad! For you know what it indicates – a mind that has lived on words and explanations, a mind that has been made dull and therefore cannot see quickly, immediately, the truth of something, but you think you will understand the truth when it is explained. Explanation and definition only make the mind more dull. I will give you a brief explanation, but the explanation is not the fact. Don't stay with the explanation, spit it out as something which doesn't taste good.)

Thought is time, and thought is fear. You must understand this, not verbally but actually, for when you come upon the immense question of death, to understand it, live it, see the whole beauty of it, thought as time must be understood, thought as fear must be understood. There was a happy experience yesterday and thought says, 'I hope I will have that experience again tomorrow.' Look at what has happened: you had a pleasurable experience yesterday and you want it repeated tomorrow; thought retains that experience as memory and thought wants that experience repeated the next day. That is what you do with regard to sex – the experience of yesterday you want repeated tomorrow. Thought has created yesterday and tomorrow. But tomorrow is uncertain; tomorrow may be something entirely different. All that thought really knows is yesterday. So thought is of yesterday, thought is old, never new.

Thought – which is experience, knowledge, the stored up bundle of memories from which thinking is the reaction –

creates time as yesterday. I was very happy yesterday, I looked at that marvellous sunset, the sun glowing, setting in the splendid sea and the cloud that passed by full of rosy colour, great beauty – there it was and now it is a memory, and tomorrow I will go there and the sun may set without colour, without such beauty. Thought has created time, as yesterday and tomorrow. That is very simple. So does thought create the fear of death? Tomorrow, in the future, there is going to be an end because you have seen death so often in the street; you know of death, there it is, walking every day by your side. And thought thinks of it as in the future, at some time to come; so there is the interval, the time, between living and dying. That interval, that time, is fear. That time, that interval, is created by thought.

We know life and we know of death. We know the life that we lead – a life of conflicts, strife, misery, aching hearts, without love and beauty – and there is that thing called death, the sudden ending. Man has invented various theories as to what happens after death; the whole of Asia believes in reincarnation; that is merely a hope, for if that belief was actually part of your life, then you would live rightly today, your acts and thoughts would be virtuous, you would be kind, generous, affectionate, because, if you were not, then in the next life you would pay for it – which is what reincarnation teaches. But you don't believe it, it is just an idea, a hope – hope to man who is afraid. So you have to re-examine the whole thing, re-examine your beliefs. Beliefs, under any circumstances, have no value at all.

A man who has a belief is a frightened man. The life that one leads – the emptiness, the misery, the sorrow, the never-ending conflict – is a battlefield; and that is all we know. That battlefield and the fear of the ending of that battlefield, which we call death, is all we know. So we have to investigate, explore, think anew, look at it anew so that a new mind can come thereby.

Can sorrow end? – which means, can fear end? When

ou cry at someone's death, are you crying for yourself or for another? Have you ever cried for another? Do please listen. Have you ever cried for another? – cried for that poor woman or man in the street with one cloth, so filthy; have you ever cried for him? Have you ever cried for your son who is killed on the battlefield? You have cried, but is that cry out of self-pity, or have you cried because a human being has been killed? If you cry out of self-pity, your tears have no meaning because you are concerned about yourself; and 'yourself' is a bundle of memories, experiences, the past tradition; you are crying because you have been bereft of him in whom you had invested a great deal of your affection – it wasn't really affection. You cry for your brother who dies, cry for *him*, not for yourself. It is very easy to cry for yourself because he is gone. Have you ever asked yourself what happened to him, why did he die? I know all the answers you are going to give me. You will say he died of disease, accident; it is his karma, it is his lot, he didn't live properly: explanations, explanations, explanations. Are you crying for explanations, or are you crying for another human being? Have you ever been concerned for another? Please, you have to answer these questions for yourself, for you have become so worldly, so utterly callous. And if you cried for another, then you would do something. But if you cry for yourself, out of self-pity, you become more callous. Although you apparently cry because your heart is touched, it is not touched, except by self-pity. Self-pity makes you hard, encloses you, it makes you dull, stupid; that is what human beings have become, because they have shed tears over themselves, over their lot, and their lot is always small compared to something else.

The ending of sorrow is the beginning of wisdom; wisdom comes naturally, easily, when there is self-knowing. It comes when you know that you are merely crying for yourself, crying out of self-pity because you are lonely, because you have been left. Always *you* in tears; if you understand that, *understand it*, which means that you come directly into contact with it – as you would touch a tree, as you would touch that pillar or a hand – then you will see that sorrow is self-centred; *you will see that sorrow is created by thought*, and is the outcome of time. I lost my son years ago, he is dead; now I am lonely, there is no one to whom I can look for comfort, for companionship; it brings tears to my eyes, which is my self-pity, and I am really not concerned at all about my son. If I had been, I would have seen to it that he lived rightly, was given right food, right exercise, right education, that he was capable of standing alone, that he was a free man. But you didn't care. You don't cry for another, you cry for your own petty, shoddy little self, which has become so extraordinarily clever in its shoddiness. You can see all this happening inside yourself – and you *can* see it, if you watch it – you can see it fully, completely, with one glance. You can see the whole structure at one glance, not taking time over it, not analysing it; you can see the nature of this shoddy little thing called 'me', 'my' tears, 'my' family, 'my' nation, 'my' belief, 'my' religion, 'my' country – all that ugliness, it is all inside you. You can see, therefore, that you are responsible for every war, for every brutality that is going on in this country, and in other countries. When you see all that with your heart, not with your mind, when you really see it from the very bottom of your heart, then you have the key that will end sorrow. Such a key opens the door to a mind that is completely untouched by experience and therefore innocent, and the innocent mind is not a mind that is made innocent by thought, thought can do nothing, thought is old; the beauty of innocency is that it is always new and therefore always young – it is only that total innocency that can see the immensity, that measureless state of mind, that man has sought for centuries upon centuries.

*From* BULLETIN 29, 1976

# The Unburdened Mind

There are many problems. The house is burning, not only your particular little place but the house of everyone; it does not matter where one lives – in the Communist world or in the world of affluence or in this poverty-ridden country, the house is burning. This is not a theory, not an idea, not something the expert, the specialist, points out. There are revolts, racial conflicts, immense poverty, the explosion of population. There are no limits to cross any more – either going to the moon or in the direction of pleasure. Organized religions, with their doctrines, beliefs, dogmas and priests, have completely failed and have no meaning any more. There is war, and the peace that the politician is trying to bring about is no peace at all.

Do you see all this? – not as a theory, not as something pointed out for you to accept or to reject, but as something from which you cannot possibly escape, by resort either to some monastery or to some past traditional ideation. The challenge is there for you to answer: it is your responsibility. You have to act, you have to do something entirely different; and, if possible, find out if there is a new action, a new way of looking at the whole phenomenon of existence.

You cannot possibly look at these problems with an old mind, living a conditioned, nationalistic, individualistic life. The word 'individual' means a being that is not divided, that is indivisible. But individuals are divided in themselves; they are fragmented, they are in contradiction. What you are, society is and the world is. So the world is you, not something apart, outside you. And when you observe this phenomenon throughout the world, the confusion that is

148

created by the politicians with their lust for power, and by the priest turning back to his old responses, muttering a few words in Latin, or Sanskrit, Greek or English, you have no faith or trust in anything or anybody any more. The more you observe outwardly what is going on and the more you observe inwardly, the less trust you have in anything, nor have you confidence in yourself.

So the question is whether it is at all possible to throw away immediately all conditioning. That means, as the crisis is extraordinary, you must have a new mind, a new heart, a new quality in the mind, a new freshness, an innocency. And that word 'innocency' means an inability to be hurt. It is not a symbol, it is not an idea; it is actually to find out if your mind is capable of not being hurt by any event, by any psychological strain, pressure, influence, so that it is completely free. If there is any form of resistance, then it is not innocency. It must be a mind that is capable of looking at this crisis as though for the first time, with a fresh mind, a young mind, yet not a mind that is in revolt. Students are in revolt against the pattern, the established order, but the revolt does not answer the human problem, which is much vaster than the revolt of the student.

Can the mind, which is heavily conditioned, break through, so that it has great depth, a quality which is not the result of training, propaganda, of acquired knowledge? And can the heart, which is burdened with sorrow, which is heavy with all the problems of life – the conflicts, the confusion, the misery, the ambition, the competition – can that heart know what it means to love? Love that has no jealousy, no envy, that is not dictated to by the intellect, love that is not merely pleasure. Can the mind be free to observe, to see? Can the mind reason logically, sanely, objectively, and not be a slave to opinions, to conclusions? Can the mind be unafraid? Can the heart know what it means to love? – not according to social morality, for social morality is immorality. You are all very moral according to society, but you are really very immoral people. Don't smile. That is a fact. You can be ambitious, greedy, envious, acquisitive, full of hate, anger, and that is considered perfectly moral. But if you are sexual, that is considered something abnormal, and you keep it to yourself. And you have patterns of actions and ideas – what things you should do, how a sannyasi should behave, that he must not marry, that he must lead a life of celibacy; this is all sheer nonsense.

Now how are you to confront this issue? What should you do? First of all, you have to realize that you are all slaves to words. The words 'to be' have conditioned your mind. Your whole conditioning is based on that verb 'to be': I was, I am, I will be. The 'I was' conditions and shapes the 'I am', which controls the future. All your religions are based on that. All your conceptual progress is based on that term 'to be'. The moment you use the word, not only verbally but with significance, you inevitably assert being as 'I am' – 'I am God', 'I am the everlasting', 'I am a Hindu or a Muslim'. The moment you live within that idea or within that feeling of being or becoming or having been, you are a slave to that word.

The crisis is in the present. The crisis is never in the future, nor in the past: it is in the present, in the living, actual present of the mind, which is conditioned by that term 'to be' and is incapable of meeting the problem. The moment you are caught in that word and the meaning of that word, you have time. And you think time will solve the problem. Are you following all this, not verbally, but in your heart, in your mind, in your being? – because it is a matter of tremendous meaning and value and importance. Because the moment you are free of that word and of the significance of what is behind that word – the past, of having been – which conditions the present and shapes the future, then your response to the present is immediate.

If you really understand this, there is an extraordinary revolution in your outlook. This is really meditation, to be free of that movement of time.

How can the mind, being aware of itself, perceive the truth of this? – not intellectually, for that has no meaning whatsoever. You know that when there is danger, your whole response to the danger is immediate. You see a bus hurtling towards you, and your response is immediate. When you say, 'I will love,' it is not love. Please don't accept this as a theory or as an idea to think about. You don't think about danger. There is no time, there is only action. A mind that is no longer thinking in terms of time, which is 'to be', is acting out of time. And the crisis demands action which is not of time.

This is one of the most difficult things. Don't say you have understood it. Don't say let us get on with it, because on those words 'I am', your whole culture is based. The moment you have this feeling 'I am', you must be in contradiction, in division – 'I am' and 'you are', 'we and they'. The moment division takes place, a fragmentation in the assertion that 'you are', you are no longer an individual – that is, a single, whole unit. Do you know what that word 'whole' means? Whole means healthy and it also means holy. So the individual who is wholly undivided in himself is healthy, holy, which means he is not in conflict.

Are you working as hard as the speaker, or are you merely listening to words? To communicate means to build, to create together, and that is the beauty of communication. And that ceases when the speaker becomes an authority and you are listening merely as students or disciples. There is no teacher, no disciple. There is only learning. What you have learnt is of the past, and acting from what has been accumulated is a process of acquisition, whereas learning should be a movement, not an accumulation.

If you understood this with your heart and mind, you would lead a different kind of life. The test and the proof of learning are your life. A mind which is facing this crisis is always new, fresh, full of vitality. But if you are responding to it in terms of 'I am', in terms of the past, then your response is going to create more misery, more mischief, more wars. So long as you are a Hindu, a Muslim, so long as you assert that 'I am', you are bringing about degeneration in yourself and in the world.

What is the new quality of the mind and the heart that responds immediately, not in terms of the past, not in terms of the future? The moment it responds in terms of the past, it is still living in the framework of the term 'to be'. Let me put it differently. Our action is based on idea, knowledge, tradition; it is memory. In the technological world that is necessary. The whole of scientific knowledge, the development of technology, is based on experience, accumulation and knowledge. That is absolutely necessary. But a mind that has a new quality, a new dimension, a new way, must act without the past and not in terms of the future – which means freedom.

How is that freedom to act to come about? How is the mind to act without the past – the past being the conditioning as a Hindu, the past being the result of influence, education, race? If you act in these terms, then you are not meeting the crisis. The question is: how is a mind to act that is free from the past, free from the implication of 'to be'?

If you have understood the question, then you will see that what is important is perception, the seeing, observing. If there is an interval between perception and action, that interval is time. When you see danger, which may cause harm physically, your response is instant; there is no thinking about it. There is no interval between perception and action, no gap; there is immediate response and action.

Now seeing that a problem cannot be solved from the past, that in no circumstance can one respond fully, wholly to this immense challenge in terms of the past, seeing this, the action that emerges is completely new. Have you understood? Do you see that response? Or do you see it only intellectually, which means verbally? If you see it verbally you are seeing it fragmentarily, and therefore it is not a whole response. But if you actually see the danger of your conditioning, of the culture in which you have been brought up, there is the immediate action of freedom.

Now, the mind – by the mind we mean the totality in which there is no fragmentation at all as the intellect, as the brain, as ambition, as sentiment, but the whole – such a mind sees the danger of nationalism, of this absurdity called religion. It sees that all the so-called religious people are repeating in terms of the past, with the image they have of the Christ, or of the Buddha or of the Krishna; it sees that if you act according to the past, you are not only adding to the confusion, to the misery, you are utterly degenerating. Degeneracy comes in only when you see the danger and do not act.

If you see the danger, you will act; and it is only the mind that sees, listens, learns that is always happy. Therefore, there is never action, but acting. In acting, the active principle – there is no division and hence no conflict. Learning is in movement and that which is in movement is free. But a mind that has conclusions, formulas, opinions, judgements, commitments, is not a free mind; when it meets the immense, complex problem of living, it is incapable of meeting it wholly, completely, with that feeling of sacredness.

So that is the thing that is in front of you. The house is burning and all your attempts in terms of the past will not put that fire out. The putting-out of that fire demands a new quality of the mind and a vital movement of the heart which is completely different.

Love is not pleasure. Love is not desire. This is the quality which you must have – now, not tomorrow – a quality which you cannot possibly practise, which you cannot possibly cultivate. That which you practise, cultivate, becomes mechanical.

Truth is not yours or mine; it is in no temple, no church,

it is not in an image, it is not in a symbol. It is there for you to see and know. It is a free mind – the lovely, clear, perceptive mind – that sees and acts.

*From* BULLETIN 17, 1973

# The Light of Compassion

MADRAS, INDIA, 1970

We are concerned with the transformation, psychologically, inwardly, of human beings. Unless our consciousness undergoes a radical transformation psychologically, there is no hope for man. This is a serious thing – to take a journey together into this whole problem of our daily existence and see if it is possible to transform, to bring about a radical, psychological revolution in the very structure of our thinking, of our acting, of our behaviour and our outlook. We are concerned with our own lives, understanding our lives, our daily miserable, conflicting, unhappy lives, and seeing if we cannot possibly bring about a deep, abiding transformation in ourselves.

Together the speaker and you are going to explore the problem of the brain, our human brain which has been damaged – so deformed, so distorted – through constant pressure of propaganda, of culture, by our ambitions, by our grief, anxiety, fears, and also by our pleasures. There has been constant pressure on the brain. That is a fact. And when there is pressure on the brain, there must be distortion unless the brain has the capacity to renew itself, can come back to itself after the pressure is over, which very few people are capable of.

There is the art of listening, the art of observation, seeing, and the art of learning. Perhaps through this art of listening, observing, learning, the pressure on the brain may never be felt at all, so that the brain remains pristine, pliable, young, fresh, innocent. It is only a mind that is innocent, that can see the truth. Pressures occur on the brain when there is ambition, violence or resistance, anger, propaganda, tradition – all these are tremendous pressures on the brain. Therefore a brain that lives under these pressures must inevitably be distorted, deformed and damaged. Through the understanding of 'what is' in the art of listening, the art of seeing, the art of learning, in capturing the full significance of these three arts, these pressures can be understood and the brain remain unaffected.

One can observe the effect of various forms of pressure on the brain. A brain that is damaged is caught in illusion, and it may meditate for a thousand years but it will not find truth. It is very important to understand whether a brain that has been so damaged can be brought back to its original quality of freshness, clarity, capable of instant decision, not based on logic, reason. Reason, logic, have a certain value, but they are limited. What we are doing now together, if you are aware of this pressure, is to be cognizant, to be conscious of it, but to know for ourselves whether our conscious thinking is the result of various pressures, and that therefore thinking is the outcome of a distorted brain. Then the problem arises whether it is possible to bring the brain back to its original condition undamaged, and therefore able to function freely. We say it is possible only when you understand or learn the art of listening, how to listen, when there is resistance to what is being said; that resistance is the outcome of your pressure. To learn the art of listening is very simple.

There is a great miracle in listening when there is no interpretation of what you are hearing, no turning it into an idea and pursuing that idea, for then you are off the mark entirely. But if you listen with your heart, with care, with attention, then that very listening is like a flowering. There is beauty in that listening. In the same way to observe the world as it is, the outer world, with all the misery, povery, degradation, vulgarity, the brutality and the appalling things that are going on in the scientific world, in the technological world, in the world of religious organizations, the crookedness, the ambition, money and power – to observe all this without bringing in your personal condemnation or acceptance, or denial, just to observe it without verbalizing it, without wanting to see beauty, just to observe. And then to observe equally that which is going on inwardly, your thoughts, your ambitions, your greed, your violence, your vulgarity, your sexuality – just observe, and then you will see, if you so observe, that your greed and all that flowers and dies, and there is an end to it.

Also there is an art of learning. Learning implies generally for most of us accumulation of knowledge stored up in the brain like a computer and acting according to that knowledge. We are introducing something entirely different, which is to learn without accumulation. To learn means to have an insight into the fact. Insight implies grasping the full significance of, for instance, your greed, grasping the full nature and the structure of greed, having an insight into it, a total comprehension of that reaction called greed. When you have an insight there is no need to learn. You are beyond it. It is very important to understand these three acts – observing, listening and learning – because if you have captured the full significance of the three, then the pressure on the brain can be understood and removed as you go along. And pressure exists on the brain when there is no space in the brain.

Everything exists in space – the trees, the fish, the clouds, the stars, the birds and human beings. They must have some space to live. The world is getting overpopulated, space is becoming rather limited. That is an obvious fact, and it may be that the pressure on human beings not having enough space, living in a city, in a town, is one of the factors of violence. And, inwardly, we have hardly any space at all. That is, our brains are so occupied, our minds are so concerned with ourselves, with our progress, with our status, with our power, with our money, with our sex, with our anxiety, that the very occupation prevents space. All our inner world is in a state of constant occupation with something or other. There is no space and because there is no space the pressure of occupation becomes greater and greater, and therefore the brain becomes more and more damaged. It is only when you have leisure that you can learn. But when the brain or the mind is so occupied, you have no leisure, so you never learn anything new. No fresh air can come in, and therefore the damage to the brain through pressure becomes greater and greater. That is one of the problems of meditation – whether the consciousness can be free from all pressure, which means a mind that is free.

We are investigating into what meditation is, not how to meditate. That is the most silly question you can possibly think of – tell me how to meditate. That means you want a system of meditation. For the speaker, there is no system of meditation. In meditation the act of will has to come totally to an end. Will is the essence of desire, a heightened form of desire. We act all our lives through will: 'I will do this', 'I must not do that', 'I will become something great'. The very essence of will is ambition, violence. Is it possible to act in daily life without the act of will, which means without control?

Is it possible to act in life, in daily life, without will, without control? The controller is the essence of desire, varying from time to time. Therefore, there is always conflict between the controller and the controlled. When traditionally you accept meditation, you try to concentrate, try to control your thoughts. In meditation, if you pursue it to its utmost depth and height, the mind must be completely free of all action of will. The action of will exists when there is choice. When there is a choice, there is confusion. Only when you are confused, you begin to choose. Only when you are clear, there is no choice. So, choice, will, control, go together and prevent the total freedom of the mind. That is one point.

The other is that you think your particular consciousness is different from mine or from another. Is that so? Your consciousness contains all the culture that has been poured into that mind, the tradition, the books that you have read, the struggle, the conflict, the misery, the confusion, the vanities, the arrogance, the cruelties, grief, sorrow, pleasure – all that is your consciousness as a Hindu, as a Buddhist, as a Muslim. The content of that makes your consciousness. Now is it possible to be free of the content? Can the mind, consciousness as we know it, be free of its content? It is very important to understand this, not how to empty consciousness of its content, but to become aware of it first. Awareness implies to observe the world as it is, to know the world, the trees, nature, the beauty and the ugliness, to be aware of your neighbour, what he or she is wearing, and also to be aware of what you are, inwardly. And if you are so aware, you will see that there are a great many reactions, like and dislike, punishment and reward, in that awareness. Can you be aware without any choice, a choiceless awareness, just to be aware without choosing, without prejudice? To become totally aware of your consciousness – which means, can consciousness become aware of itself? Which means also can thought, your thinking, become aware of itself?

The brain is like a computer. It is registering, registering your experiences, your hopes, your desires, your ambitions; it is registering every impression, and from that impression, from that registration, thought arises. Now, we are asking, can there be an awareness of thought arising, as you can be aware of your anger arising? You can be aware of it, can't you? As one can be aware of anger rising, so can you be aware of thought beginning? Which means to be aware of the thing flowering, growing. In the same way, is there an awareness of your consciousness, the totality of it? This is part of meditation. This is the essence of meditation – to be aware, without any choice, of the world outside you, and the immense conflict of the world inside you. When you come to this point, you will see that the world is not separate from you; the world is you. By consciousness becoming aware of itself, the parts that make up consciousness disappear. Then consciousness becomes quite a different thing. Then it is consciousness of the whole, not of the part.

Most of us are accustomed to systems, various forms of yoga, various forms of government, various forms of bureaucratic rule, and they are all based on systems. Your guru will give you a system of meditation; or you pick up a book and learn from that book a system. System implies the comprehension of the whole through the part. By studying the part, you hope to understand the totality of existence. Your brain, your mind, is trained to follow systems, political systems, religious systems, yogic systems or your own systems. When you are following a system you are stuck in a groove, and that is the easiest way to live. A system is like a railway track, and followers of a system are unaware that they are like the train on the track that keeps going, confined to the lines.

So concentration is resistance to all other forms of thought. You cultivate resistance, whereas we are saying that concentration at a certain level only is necessary. Even there, if we can learn how to attend, concentration becomes very easy. We are going to find out what it means to attend, to give your heart, your mind, all your senses completely to something. When you so attend, when all your senses are completely awakened and observing, then in that process or in that quality of attention there is no centre. When there is no centre, there is no limitation to space. Most of us have a centre, which is the form of the 'me', the ego, the personality, the character, the tendency, the idiosyncrasy, the peculiarities and so on. There is a centre in each one, which is the essence of the self, which is selfishness. Wherever there is a centre, the space must always be limited. That is why we are saying a mind that is occupied is forming a centre all the time, and therefore its occupation is limiting the space. When there is total attention, when you observe, hear, learn, with all your senses awakened, there is no centre.

Do it in daily life, in your relationship with your wife, with your neighbour, in your relationship with nature. Relationship means to be related. You can only be related to another if you have no image about yourself or about another; then you are directly related.

Out of this comes compassion; that is, passion for all. That can only take place when there is this perfume, this quality of love, which is not desire, which is not pleasure, which is not the action of thought. Love is not a thing put together by thought, by environment, by sensation. Love is not emotion, love is not sensation. Love means the love of rocks, love of trees, love of a stray dog, love of the skies, the beauty, the sunset, love of your neighbour, love without all the sensation of sexuality with which it is identified now. Love cannot exist when you are ambitious, when you are seeking power, position, money. How can a man love you, if you are the wife, when all his mind is concentrated on becoming something, on having power in the world? He can sleep with you, have children, but that is not love. That is lust, with all its misery. And without love, you cannot have compassion. When there is compassion, there is clarity, the light that comes from compassion. Every act is clear, and from that clarity comes skill, skill in communication, skill in action, skill in the art of listening, learning, observing.

Meditation is the awakening of that intelligence that is born out of compassion, clarity and the skill that intelligence uses. That intelligence is non-personal, non-cultivable; it comes only out of compassion and clarity. All this is meditation and much more, and the more is when the mind is free and therefore completely quiet. It cannot be quiet if there is no space. So, silence can come, not through practice, not through control, not between two noises, not the peace

between two wars; silence comes only when the body and
the mind are in complete harmony without any friction.
Then, in that silence there is a total movement which is the
end of time. That means time has come to an end. There is
much more in meditation, which is to find that which is
most sacred; not the sacredness of the idols of the temples or
in the churches or the mosques – those are man-made,
handmade, made by the mind, by thought. There is sacredness which is not touched by thought. That can only come
about naturally, easily and happily when we have brought
about complete order in our daily life. When there is such
order in our daily life – order means no conflict – then out
of that comes this quality of love, compassion and clarity.
And meditation is all this – not an escape from life, from
your daily living. And those who know the quality of this
meditation are blessed.

*From* BULLETIN 45, 1983

# On Meditation

INDIA, 1970

The human mind, which has lived for many thousands of years, should radically change and uncondition itself. Only then can the many complex problems of existence be resolved. Can the mind undergo a radical surgery, a fundamental mutation, not only of the structure of the brain cells themselves but also of the quality of the heart and the mind? Can such a mind live in the midst of chaos, of brutality and violence, which modern society is, free to function undisturbed, quietly, without any possible resistance, but without withdrawal from society?

One observes the tremendous necessity to bring about a fresh mind, not the mind that has had a thousand experiences, or is caught in the pattern of a particular religious, social or economic culture. This pattern is being endlessly repeated throughout history, changing a little bit here and there. The economic and social revolutions are really no revolutions at all. As a human being, living a meaningless existence in this world of confusion, in this world of great sorrow, of ugliness, of violence, one wonders whether the human mind can really transform itself. In that alone is the solution of all our problems, of love, of reality, of whether there is or is not God or truth, of whether human beings can live together without conflict. To find this out actually with your heart, with your being, there must be freedom – freedom to look, to inquire, to perceive. That surely is the first thing – freedom to observe – because that freedom is denied when there is any form of prejudice, conclusion, any ideation, belief and above all any fear.

If there is any form of fear, obviously the whole totality

of the mind is incapable of seeing. We have gone to the moon; that is an extraordinary achievement. Our brains are capable of it. But inwardly we are slaves, and there is no freedom; we repeat the same pattern thousands of times, sociologically, religiously, economically. And in the psyche, in the very depth of our being, there is no change at all. We are modern monsters.

Is the mind ever capable of this tremendous, immediate revolution, so that it can live with a new quality, so that there is not this drive for pleasure, which is entirely different from the beauty and the flowering of joy? Pleasure is never joyous, because in pleasure there is always fear. And a mind that is not ecstatic cannot be free. Pleasure is the product of thought, and thought is always old; thought is never new, thought is never free, though one may talk about freedom. Thought cannot at any level be free, because thought is the response of memory and memory is always of the past. It has its roots in time, which is of the past. Please observe this in yourself as the speaker is talking about it, don't merely agree or disagree – that has no value.

The human mind, which is so astonishingly capable, has never set out to find out for itself whether it can ever be free – free, essentially, from fear, because we are burdened with innumerable fears. To find out, one must observe the fears one has – not condemn them, repress them or escape from them. In the observation there is no division between the observer and the thing observed. Observe them without the past, the 'me', who is the observer.

Do try it, as the speaker is talking about it, because we are going into something very complex this evening. If you don't do this at the beginning, you won't follow what is going to come at the end. (I do not know what is going to come at the end either.) A mind that is frightened cannot possibly be acute, clear, unconfused, and therefore it can never know what the quality of joy is, or of ecstasy.

There must be freedom from fear, not only at the conscious level, but in the deep layers of the mind in which the so-called unconscious is. Most of us are incapable of analysing ourselves step by step so that we are very clear; we must take a little journey into it to see the utter futility of it. The whole process of analysis is entirely wrong, if we may use that word 'wrong'. Because, in that, there is always the analyser, who is the past, who is the accumulated knowledge; and he, a fragment of the totality of the mind, is analysing other fragments, analysing from what he has accumulated. To observe the analytical movement in oneself, taking a very short journey into it and seeing the utter futility of it, gives the mind a quality of perception.

The analyser and the analysed are two separate states, two separate movements of the total fragmentation of the mind. One fragment, called the analyser, analyses the other fragment, comes to a conclusion and from that conclusion analyses further. But the conclusion has very little value. And the analysis implies time, because it takes many, many days to analyse.

Introspective analysis, or analysis by another through dreams and so on, has little meaning. If you are slightly or greatly neurotic, then there is perhaps a little meaning in helping you to adjust yourself to your rotten society, whether the Communist society or your own particular Hindu society. So the analysis does not bring freedom at all. It is like digging more and more into oneself and being caught in a pit; one never becomes free. Or the mind says there is freedom in heaven or nirvana, which, again, is an evasion.

To observe without any distortion is only possible if there is complete attention with your body, your nerves, your mind, your heart, your ears. Then you will see, if you so attend, that there is no entity or being called the observer. Then there is only attention.

The very substance and the nature of the brain is to survive – that is obvious. The brain insists on survival, otherwise you cannot exist; and it has developed certain responses from centuries and centuries of conditioning. What we are trying to inquire into is whether the very structure and nature of the brain can bring about a change in itself. And we will show you – not show you – we are going to learn together, if that is possible. This is not an absurdity, or fanciful imagination, because imagination has no place whatsoever when you are inquiring tremendously deeply; there is no theory, no conclusion, but only moving from fact to fact.

The quality of the mind must be extraordinarily sensitive – and it cannot be sensitive if there is fear, if there is any conclusion, dogma, belief – so that the brain itself, which is so heavily conditioned, can be completely quiet and not respond according to its own traditional way. The question is how to bring about a quality of sensitivity to the mind and therefore to the whole nervous system and the body, and also to bring about a non-movement of the brain cells, a complete quietness, for the mind to be awake, highly intelligent, sensitive. Awake and intelligent and sensitive: they are all synonymous, not three separate things. And the brain must be utterly quiet so that it perceives without the observer. This is meditation, to see the brain quiet, completely quiet, and a mind that is highly sensitive and therefore intelligent. To come upon this movement is meditation.

Can there be a system for meditation, a system being a method, a practice, the repetition of something over and over again? Does that make the mind sensitive, alive, active, intelligent? On the contrary, it makes the mind mechanical.

Therefore any system, the Zen system, the Hindu system or the Christian system, is all nonsense. A mind which practises a system, a method, a mantra, is not capable of perceiving what is true. You know you are hearing that music [the sound of music was being heard from the next compound]. There is a tone and if you listen to it very carefully, listen to it – not to the words, but to the tonality, the sound – that sound can be produced within yourselves. And the mind can ride on that movement of the tone, of the sound, and that gives you an extraordinary sense of movement. And that may be called meditation, a repetition of a set of words which produces the sound, an inward sound, and you can move or ride or be with that sound.

But is that meditation, playing a trick like that, mesmerizing yourself by a sound or by words? Such forms of meditation are forms of self-hypnosis. It does not lead you anywhere. On the contrary, it makes the mind extraordinarily dull, a mind that is not moral in the deepest sense of that word – not social morality, which is no morality at all.

The quality of virtue can only be when there is no conflict whatsoever. Then there is virtue. But a man who is trying to become virtuous is deadened because he is living in conflict. You can discard all the systems, because systems imply authority; a mind that is held by authority of any kind is not free and therefore is incapable of observing. In so-called meditation, in the meditation that is generally practised, there is always the desire to experience truth, various visions, states and so on.

Experience implies an experiencer, an entity as the experiencer. Therefore when he experiences, he must recognize what he experiences; otherwise it is not an experience. And when he recognizes, it is already known; therefore the experience is of the past. The mind seeks experience through drugs – as it is the fashion now in the West – drugs of various kinds in order to have great trips into heaven. There must be, there is always, the experiencer who is craving, searching, longing, hoping for experience, transcendental, super-cosmic and what not.

And when you are seeking experiences, you will always find them within the pattern, within the conditioning of the mind of the experiencer. So there is a division between the experiencer and the thing experienced and therefore always a searching, wanting, groping, a conflict. And we say that that is not meditation. The highest form of sensitivity with the brain completely still is the quality of love. You know love is a most extraordinary thing if you have it in your heart. Love is not pleasure. Love has nothing to do with fear. It is not related to sex. It is the quality of the mind that is free, sensitive, intelligent with the brain not responding in terms of the past and therefore still. Then the heart comes upon this perfume called love. The understanding of that is meditation. That is the foundation of meditation.

Without it there is no virtue; virtue is a movement in which there is no conflict whatsoever. And there must be that freedom, that sense of love, to find out for yourself if there is or is not a reality, if there is or is not that thing which human beings have called for centuries upon centuries God; to find out, not to say, 'I believe in God,' as does the ugly corrupt politician; it pays him. But the description is not the described. And to find out that timeless quality, that timeless movement, there must be energy and no conflict, the energy that is astonishingly awakened and intelligent. And therefore meditation is not a thing that can be practised. Meditation is the way of life, meditating all day, looking, observing, moving, learning. And to observe that, there must be a still mind.

The innumerable problems of life, the economic, and the social injustice, the conflict between man and man, and woman and man, the conflict between groups and social divisions, the division of religions – all those have little meaning. A revolution, the inward revolution of the mind, is necessary to answer all those problems. And meditation in the way we have described is necessary to understand this extraordinarily complex life.

We are human beings, not labels, and as human beings living in this miserable sorrow-laden world, we have to understand it, our relationship to it, our contact with it. We are the world, the world is not separate from us. The wars that are going on are our wars because we human beings have contributed to them. You have to understand this observer which is you, to understand yourself, not through analysis. In that observation you will find that acting is seeing. Only such a mind can find out for itself whether there is a reality or not. It has no speculation, no theories, no books, no teachers, no disciples. And such a mind is a mind that is aware of ecstasy.

*From* BULLETIN 7, 1970

# *Freedom*

SAANEN, SWITZERLAND, 19 JULY 1973

Knowing what the world is, which each one of us has created, with all its fragmentation and division, with its brutalities, chicanery, deceptions, violence and wars and all the horrors that are going on, we have two central problems. First, is it possible to turn our back on this world – that is, to turn away from the culture, the civilization, all that man has put together throughout the centuries, and free the mind from that conditioning? That is one issue. Secondly, is it possible in the very process of unconditioning the mind to live in this world, yet not of it, not involved in it?

I do not know if you have considered how serious this is. It is not an entertainment, something that one seeks out of pleasure, or out of despair, but rather, being aware of the whole situation, the various intricacies in the world movement, historically, outwardly and inwardly, these questions are a matter of urgent concern. Man has destroyed nature, exterminated certain species of animals and birds. He has created the most beautiful cathedrals, mosques and temples, great literature, music, painting. And that is part of our culture, the beauty, the ugliness, the cruelty, the immense destruction of man by man. That is part of our civilization, of which we are part. I do not know if you really fully realize what is involved in all this, economically, socially, religiously. If you have examined it in some depth, you must be concerned with whether the structure can be changed, the structure that has created this world; you must have asked what has brought about this structure, and whether by merely changing the structure man will be changed? This has been one of the theories of the world:

change the outer conditions, then man will be changed inwardly – that has always been one of the arguments. But you see that it doesn't work that way. So it is man who has to change and thereby change the structure.

Now can the mind, your mind, be free from this culture? And what does it mean to be free from culture? Is it a matter of analysis? Is it a matter of time? Is it a matter of more rational, logical conclusions of thought? Or is it a non-movement of thought? Please go into this with me a little bit. It may be somewhat difficult – you may not be used to this kind of thinking, you may not have thought about it at all. So please have a little patience and thereby share together this extraordinary question. Can this conditioning of the mind, which has been brought about through time, experience and knowledge, be dissolved by analysis? That is one point.

Analysis, the very word means to break up. And through fragmentation we hope to understand and dissolve the complex problem of conditioning, both at the conscious and the unconscious level. Can this be done through analysis, between the analyser and the analysed, taking months, years? All that involves time, and by that time you will be dead! I can analyse myself very, very carefully, step by step, investigate the cause, the effect, the effect becoming the cause, which is the chain in which analysis is caught. Can the mind analyse itself and dissolve all its peculiarities, violence, superstitions, the various contradictions, and thereby bring about a total harmony?

As we said, analysis implies time, and what is time? Time is both a physical and a psychological movement – physically, a movement from here to there, psychologically a movement from 'what is' to 'what should be', transforming 'what is' through an ideology, which is a movement in time. Right? Please, we are sharing this question together, not you just listening to me; we are travelling together, investigating, together finding out what is true. It is not for you to accept what the speaker is saying; that has no value whatsoever, neither verbally nor in reality. What has reality is when we, through investigation, through observation, through very careful awareness, share that which we discover for ourselves. That has validity; it has substance, meaning. There is no significance in merely listening to a series of words and translating these into ideas, and then putting these ideas into action.

So, as we are saying, time is movement. Physically moving from here to there takes time. Psychologically it is also a movement, moving from 'what is' and changing to 'what should be'. 'What is', which is the result of the past, is a movement in time to the present, and 'what should be' is a movement into the future. The whole movement is time. Right? And thought is always a process in time, for thought is the response of memory, which is the past, based on knowledge which is also the past, and according to that conditioning it reacts, which is a movement. So thought is a movement in time. And analysis is a movement in time, the movement of thought examining itself. And we are conditioned to analyse. You will see, if you go into it deeply, that that is our conditioning. We never see that the cause becomes the effect, and the effect becomes the cause. That is a movement in time. Analysis does not free the mind, which is the result of time.

I wonder if you see this? It is fairly simple if you observe it in yourself. I am angry. I analyse the cause, and in the process of analysis I come to a conclusion, which is the effect. And that conclusion becomes the cause of the next effect. All that is a movement of thought in time. Thought *is* time. And thought has built this conditioning. All our culture is the result of thought, as feeling, physical responses and so on. So analysis cannot possibly resolve the conditioning of the human mind. I hope it is clear – not the verbal statement, but the truth of it, the actual fact, not the assertion or the repetition of a statement, that analysis will not free the mind. That has no value.

So the mind, seeing the falseness of analysis, discovers the truth that analysis does not free the mind – that is, it discovers the truth *in* the false. Now, analysis involves not only the conscious mind but also the deep layers of the unconscious, which is also the result of time. This division between the conscious and the unconscious is artificial. Consciousness is total. We may divide it, we may break it up to examine it, but it is a total movement within the field of time. And the unconscious loses its importance when you are able to look at the whole of consciousness and its content. You understand? We look at ourselves fragmentarily. We look at ourselves through the action of thought.

Look, sirs, my consciousness is a total movement. It can be broken up as the conscious and the unconscious, as action and inaction, as greed, envy, non-envy; but it is a totality, a total movement which can be fragmented only in order to examine it. And I see that an examination of fragments doesn't bring about a comprehension of the whole. Right? What is needed is to be aware of the whole, not merely of the fragments, to be aware of the whole movement of consciousness, which is in the area of time. Can thought, can I, as thought, explore this consciousness? You see, what I am trying to say is this: personally, I have never analysed myself at all. What has taken place is observation, and in that very observation the total is revealed because there is no intention of going beyond 'what is'. Going beyond 'what is' is the movement of time. Is that fairly clear?

So I see clearly that the mind can, without analysis, discover, observe, the total movement of consciousness. That is one point. What we are concerned with is whether the mind can free itself from its conditioning. I see it cannot free itself from its conditioning through analysis as that involves time, and to dissolve time through time is not possible. Then can thought dissolve it? Can thought transform, free the mind from its conditioning? Now please listen

173

to this. Thought is movement in time; thought is movement and therefore time. And the examination by thought of the conditioning is still within the field of time, therefore thought cannot possibly resolve the conditioning because it is thought as knowledge, experience, memory, that has brought about this civilization in which the mind has been educated. That is clear. So thought cannot resolve it. Analysis cannot. Then what have you left? You understand? We have used thought as a means of conquering, destroying, changing, analysing, overcoming. And I see that thought cannot possibly bring freedom to the mind. Thought is movement. Thus *non-movement* is freedom from time. Right? Non-movement of thought is a state in which the mind is free from time. Now, I'll go into this; you will see it.

The conditioning of civilization, culture, has emphasized that I must be competitive, has taught me to be violent, or, rather, encouraged me to be more violent. So the mind is violent; that is 'what is'. Can the mind be free of violence, which is 'what is', without the movement of thought? You understand my question? I am violent and thought says, 'Overcome that violence, control that violence, utilize that violence,' thus encouraging or controlling, shaping that violence for its own purposes. That is what we are doing all the time. So thought, being a movement, is continuously acting upon 'what is', which is also the result of time and thought. Right? Now can thought have no movement at all so that only the 'what is' remains without any interference of thought? Look, sirs, I am violent; I know all the causes, how violence has come about. That is fairly clear, it is part of the culture, encouraged by the economic situation, education and so on. I am violent, that is 'what is'. Can the mind look at 'what is' without any movement? Any movement is time. So can the mind observe that violence with non-thought, that is, without time?

Have you at least understood my question? My conditioning says, 'Use thought to control violence, to shape it, to get rid of it, to struggle against it; it is ugly to be violent, human beings should be peaceful.' So it provides all the reasons, justifications, condemnations, which are all movements of thought, and thought is time, and movement is time. Yet there is only the fact that this human being is violent. So far that is clear.

Can the mind look at 'what is' without any movement? The 'what is' is violence. Now, I have used a word to indicate a feeling which I have named 'violence', and that word with its meaning I have already used before. So I am recognizing the feeling in terms of the old. Whenever I recognize something it must be the old. So 'what is' is the result of thought. Now the mind meets without movement, which means without time, that which has been put together by thought, which I have called 'violence'. So when non-movement meets thought, which is the movement of time, then what takes place? Are you following?

Look, sirs, my son dies; I suffer a great deal for various reasons, loneliness, despair and so on. Then thought comes along and says, 'I must overcome it'. The 'what is' is suffering, and the movement of thought is time. The mind meets that suffering and tries to do something about it, to escape from it, seeks comfort in séances, in mediums, in beliefs; it goes through all that process, which is all a movement of time as thought. Now, in meeting that suffering without any movement, what takes place? Have you ever tried this? If you have, you will see that the non-movement completely transforms the movements of time, and that which we call suffering is time. That means suffering doesn't leave a mark on the mind at all because non-movement is timeless, and that cannot possibly touch that which is not of itself.

So the mind is conditioned through culture, through environment, through knowledge, through experience – all of which is the movement of time, and thought is also a movement of time. Thus thought cannot possibly transform or free the mind from its conditioning, just as analysis cannot.

The question is can the mind observe this conditioning, this educated entity, without any movement? If you do it, then you will see that all sense of control, imitation, conformity, totally disappears.

*From* BULLETIN 21, 1974

## Beyond Thought and Time

If we are seriously concerned with the transformation of the human mind and heart, we must be totally dedicated to the resolution of our problems because the content of our consciousness is the content of the world. Though there are modifications, the consciousness of each one of us is the consciousness of the rest of the world. And if there is a radical change in that consciousness, that consciousness will affect the rest of the world. That is an obvious fact. We have spent a great deal of energy in attempts to solve our problems – intellectual energy, emotional energy, physical energy – and all this energy, with its contradictions, with its conflicts, with its varying purposeful destructive activity, has not in any way resolved our human psychological problems. I think this is a fact which nobody can deny.

We are concerned to find out if there is a different kind of energy which will, if we can tap it, resolve our problems. So we are investigating together, inquiring into the possibility of a different kind of energy which is non-contradictory in itself, which is not based on the divisive activity of thought, not dependent on environment, on education, on cultural influence. We are asking if there is a different activity, a different movement which is not dependent on self-centred activities, the activities and the energies which the self, the 'me' creates with all its contradictions. Is there an energy which has no cause? Because cause implies time.

We have used only a very small area of the brain, and that small area is controlled and shaped by thought, and thought, intellectually, emotionally, physically, has created a contradictory energy, the 'me' and the 'you', 'we' and 'they', what we are and what we should be, the ideal, the perfect prototype. I hope you are following this. I think it is very important to understand that we are working together, that the speaker is not telling you what to do, because the speaker has no authority. Authority in spiritual matters has been very destructive because authority implies conformity, fear, obedience, following and accepting but when we are investigating together it means that there is no sense of following, no sense of agreeing or denying, but merely observing, inquiring. Together we are doing this. Therefore when we are together 'you' and 'I' disappear. It is the work which is important, not you or I. So we are working together to find out if there is a totally different kind of energy, which is not based on a cause that divides the action of the present from the past.

Now this inquiry implies that we are asking whether there is an area in the brain which is not contaminated by thought, which is not the product of evolution, not touched by culture. From ancient times man has used only a very small area of the brain, in which there has been conflict between the good and the bad. You can see that in all the paintings, in all the symbols, in all the activities of man. This conflict between the good and the bad, between 'what is' and 'what should be', between 'what is' and the ideal, has produced a culture, Christian, Hindu, Buddhist and so on. And by that culture this small area of the brain is conditioned. Can the mind free itself from that conditioning, from that limited area, and move into an area which is not controlled by time, by causation, by direction?

So one has to begin by finding out what is time, what is direction, and what it is human beings are trying to achieve in the psychological field. What is time psychologically? There is chronological time, by the clock, but psychologically is there time at all? Time meaning movement – right? Time also implies direction. Psychologically we say that 'what is' can only be changed through a gradual process, and that requires time. And the gradual process is in a definite direction, the direction established by the ideal. To achieve that you must have time as a movement from here to there, and in that area of time we are caught. That is, I am what I am, I must transform that into what I should be, and to do that I need the movement of time. And the direction is controlled, shaped by the ideal, by the formula, by the concept which thought has created. That is, the ideal is created by thought, the thought which says, 'I am this, and I should be that,' and the movement towards that. This is the traditional approach to the transformation of man. Now, we are questioning that altogether.

So time is a movement in a specific direction set by thought – right? And therefore we live always in conflict. This divisive process of what I am and what I should be is the very action of thought which is in itself divisive, fragmentary. Thought has divided people through nationalities, religions, 'you' and 'I', and so we are always in conflict, and we are trying to solve our problems within that area of time.

So can the mind, which is so conditioned in this tradition, break away from it and only deal with 'what is' and not with 'what should be'? To do that you need energy, and that energy comes and maintains and sustains itself where there is no movement of thought away from 'what is'. Can your mind, which is the mind of man, because you are the collective, you are not an individual – individual means indivisible, the whole, non-fragmented, not broken up, as human beings are – can your mind with its self-centred activity uncondition itself, not in the future, but instantly? Can your mind uncondition itself without the thought of time?

Time is the observer who is the past, and the observed is the present. You understand? My mind is conditioned and the observer says, 'I have all these problems and I have not been able to solve them, so I will observe my conditioning, I will be aware of it and go beyond it.' This is tradition reacting – right? So the observer, who is the past, which means he is the essence of time, is trying to overcome, transcend and go beyond what he observes, which is his conditioning. Now is the observer, who is the past, different from the thing he observes? The thing he observes is what he sees according to his conditioning – obviously. So he observes with thought which is the outcome of time, and he is trying to solve the problem through time. But one sees the observer *is* the observed.

Look, sirs, I'll put it very simply. Is violence different from the observer who says 'I am violent'? Is violence different from the actor who is violent? Surely they are both the same, aren't they? So the observer is the observed, and as long as there is a division between the observer and the observed there must be conflict. This division comes into being when the observer assumes that he is different from the observed. Get a little insight into this and you will see what is implied in it.

We live in total disorder and confusion, physically, psychologically and intellectually, confusion being contradiction: saying one thing, doing another, thinking something and acting in another way. But order is necessary for the brain to function properly, objectively. It is obvious that, like a machine, if it is not functioning properly it is useless. Now can order come out of this discovery? Order, not according to the priest or according to social order – which is immoral – but order without conflict, without control, with no admission of time at all. Can that perfect order, which is virtue, come from the observation of this disorder in which one lives? That means, can the mind observe, be aware of this disorder, not seeking how to deal with it or to transcend it, but be choicelessly aware of it? And to be choicelessly aware, the observer must not interfere with the observation. The observer, who is the past, who says, 'This is right, this is wrong, I must choose this, I must not choose that, this should be, this should not be,' must not interfere with the observation at all.

Now can you observe your disorder without the inter-ference, without the movement of thought, which is time – just observe? Observation implies attention, obviously, and when you are attending totally to disorder, is there disorder? Thus order becomes like the highest form of mathematics, which is complete order. So there is a way of living without any control, which is to observe without the movement of thought as time. Go into it and you will see this. What creates time is the division between the observer and the observed, and you have removed this division altogether when there is total attention and awareness. Therefore rela-tionship in your daily life, which we have discussed in previ-ous talks, is an actual relationship in which the image of 'you' and the image of 'her' or 'him' is non-existent. Now, having established this, which is order, we are asking whether the brain, that small area which is so controlled, so shaped by culture, by time, whether the brain, the mind, can be free of all that, yet function effectively in the field of knowledge?

Let me put it differently. Is there a part of the brain which is not touched at all by human endeavour, human violence, hope, desire and all the rest of it? You understand my question? The mind has brought about order within that small area, and without that order there is no freedom to inquire. Order means freedom, obviously. Order means security so that there is no disturbance. Now the mind says, 'I see the necessity of order, of responsibility in relationship, and so on – but the human problems are not solved.' Then the mind asks, 'Is there a different kind of energy?' You are following this? *This* is meditation – not sitting quietly, breathing in a certain way, following a system, a guru, which is all silly nonsense. Meditation is to find out if there is an area of the brain where there may be a different kind of energy, where there may be an area where time doesn't exist and therefore immeasurable space. How is the mind to find out if there is such a thing?

First, there must be doubt. Doubt is a purifying agent but it must be held in leash. You must not only doubt but also you must hold it in leash – otherwise you will doubt everything, which would be too stupid. So doubt is necessary – doubt whatever you experience, because your experience is based on the experiencer. The experiencer *is* the experience – you understand? – therefore the search for more experience becomes absurd. The mind must be very clear not to create illusions; one can imagine that one has got the new kind of energy, that one has achieved the timeless state, therefore one must be very clear about having no illusions. Now illusion comes into being only where there is a desire to achieve something – we are speaking psychologically. When I desire to achieve God, whatever that God may be, that God which I have created out of myself, there is an illusion. So I must understand very clearly this desire, and the drive and the energy which that desire promotes. So there must be doubt and no factor of illusion. Do you understand? This is very serious, this isn't a plaything. All religions have created illusions, because religions are the product of our desires, exploited by the priests.

So, to come upon that energy, if there is such energy, if there is such an immeasurable state, thought must be absolutely quiet – without control. Is that possible? Our thought is endlessly chattering, always in action: 'I want to find out if there is that state; all right, I'll doubt, I'll have no illusions, I will live a life of order because that other state may be marvellous, so I must have it.' It is chattering endlessly. Can that chatter come to an end without any control, without any suppression, because any form of suppression or control distorts the full movement of the brain? All distortion must come to an end, otherwise the brain ends up in a neurotic illusion of security.

Unless the mind can be completely quiet it cannot move into any other field, it will carry its own momentum into the other, *if* there is 'the other', because I am doubting 'the other' all the time, for the reason that I don't want to be caught in any illusion, which is so easy, so cheap and so vulgar. I am putting this problem to you to solve to exercise your capacity, your brain, to find out if your mind can be absolutely quiet, which means the ending of time, the ending of thought, without effort, control, without any form of suppression. Is your mind ever quiet? Not day-dreaming, not vacant, but quiet, attentive, aware? Haven't you known it to happen occasionally? To see anything, to hear anything the mind must be quiet, mustn't it? Your very interest in what is being said brings about this quietness of mind that will listen. I am interested in what you are talking about because it affects my life, my way of living, and I want to listen to you completely, not only through the words, the semantic movement of thought, but what lies behind. I want to find out exactly what you say, not interpret it, translate it according to my pleasure or vanity. So in my very intensity of listening to you I have to have a quiet mind. I wonder if you see this? I have not compelled my mind to be quiet; the very attention of listening to you *is* quietness. The very attention given to finding out if the mind can be completely quiet *is* quietness. And this silence of the mind is necessary; untrained silence, because trained silence is noise. It is meaningless. Therefore meditation is not a controlled, directed activity; it is an activity of 'no thought'.

Then you will find out for yourself if there is or if there is not something which is not nameable, which is not within the field of time. Without finding that out, without coming upon it, without seeing the truth of it or the falseness of it, life becomes a shallow, empty thing. You may have perfect order in yourself, you may have no conflict because you have become very alert, watchful, but all that becomes utterly superficial without the other.

So meditation, contemplation – not in the Christian sense or the Asiatic sense – means thought operating only in the field of the known and thought realizing for itself that it cannot move into any other field. Therefore the ending of thought means the ending of time.

*From* BULLETIN 25, *SPRING* 1975

# Time, Action and Fear

SAANEN, SWITZERLAND, 20 JULY 1975

We are talking over together a very serious matter, which is: can there be freedom, total freedom, from psychological fears? To go into it very deeply, one must not only understand what is time, but what is action, because action breeds fear, stored up as memory, and that memory restrains, controls, shapes action. So if you would be free of fear you must understand that fear is time. If there were no time you would have no fear. I wonder if you see that? If there were no tomorrow, only the now, fear, as a movement of thought, ends.

There is chronological as well as psychological time. In that area we live. In that area of movement of thought as time, there is action, acting as a Christian, or a Communist, a Socialist, or a Buddhist, or a Hindu, and so on, always within the movement of thought as time and measure. This is clear, I think, so we can now go into finding out what is the source of fear.

You may not be afraid of anything now, sitting here. But obviously in your consciousness there is fear. In the unconscious, or in the conscious, there is this terrible thing called anxiety, pain, grief, suffering and fear. One may be afraid psychologically of tomorrow, what might happen or what might not be achieved. Will that relationship which has given great pleasure, great comfort, continue, be permanent? Or will there be change? – which the mind dreads because the mind, the brain, needs stability, needs security to function. Please follow this. The brain will create any conclusion because that gives it security. It may be a rational or an irrational conclusion, an idiotic belief or a rational observation. The brain will cling to these because they offer action a complete sense of security.

So there are fears, conscious as well as unconscious, hidden fears in the recesses of one's own mind, which have never been explored, which have never been opened. Fear, like sorrow, is a dark cloud that distorts all action. It breeds despair, cynicism, or hope – all are irrational. And fear is the movement of thought as time, so it is real, it is not fictitious.

Now our problem is how is a mind, how are you, to unravel this fear which is so deeply hidden? Can it ever be unravelled? Or is it always there, showing its head occasionally when a crisis or some incident takes place, when a challenge is offered? Or can it be totally brought out? We have said that analysis is a process of fragmentation. When the mind realizes that there must be total freedom from fear, what is a human being to do? Shall he wait for an intimation, hints of the unconscious through dreams, take time through analysis? If you discard all that, not in theory but actually discard it because it has no meaning, then what is the totality, the whole structure of fear? If the mind can look at, can understand, the totality of fear, then the unconscious has very little importance, then the greater washes away the lesser. You don't see this? Wait a minute.

Please follow this. Thought has created the microphone, but the microphone is independent of the thought which has created it – right? The mountain is not created by thought; it is independent of thought. Fear is put together by thought. Is that thought independent of fear? Is fear independent of thought though fear has created thought? If it is independent of thought, as the mountain, then that fear not made by thought will go on living. If it is made by thought, as the microphone, then there is a perception of the whole movement of thought as fear. Does this convey anything to you?

How does one perceive the whole of anything? The whole

of fear, not the broken up fragments of fear in different forms, nor the fear of the conscious and the unconscious, but the whole of fear? How do I perceive the whole of me, the 'me' constructed by thought, isolated by thought, fragmented by thought, which in itself is fragmented, so that it creates the 'me' and thinks that the 'me' is independent of thought? The 'me' thinks it is independent of thought, but thought has created the 'me', the 'me' with all its anxieties, fears, vanities, agonies, pleasures, hopes. That 'me', created by thought, thinks it has its own life, like the microphone which is created by thought and yet is independent of thought. The mountain is not created by thought and yet it is independent. The 'me' created by thought, says, 'I am independent of thought!' Is this clear now?

So how does one see the totality of fear? To see something totally, or to listen to something completely, there must be freedom, freedom from prejudice, freedom from your conclusions, from your wanting to be free of fear; freedom from the rationalization of fear, freedom from the desire to control it. Can the mind be free of all that? Otherwise it can't see the whole. Can one look at all the fears that one has – please listen – can one look at them without any movement of thought, which is time, which causes fear? Do you understand? I am afraid of not becoming something because I have been educated, conditioned by society that says I must be something, as an artist, an engineer, a doctor, a politician, whatever you like, I must be something. And there germinates one of the seeds of fear. Then there is the fear of thought not being certain – and thought can never be certain because in itself it is a fragment. Thought can never see the whole because, being a fragment, it can only observe fragmentarily. One can describe the various forms of fear, each insoluble because they are fragmented by thought. So one asks: what is the root of fear? Can I see not only the whole tree of fear but also the root of fear?

What do you think is the root of fear, both conscious and

unconscious? If you are challenged, how do you answer?
We are challenging you. How do you respond? Do you see,
perceive, what is the total cause of this thing called fear, or
are you waiting for somebody to tell you, and then accept
it? And you say, 'Yes, I see it' – which means that you
don't actually see it. You see the description. Is time the
root of fear, the root of time being the movement of thought?
Is the source of fear uncertainty, and therefore no stability,
no security psychologically, which will affect the physical
action and therefore society? If there is complete security
psychologically there is no fear. I wonder if you see this?

So where does the mind find complete security – absolute,
not relative? Thought wants to be secure. The brain
demands complete security because it is only then that it
can function rationally. So it has sought security in knowledge, in science, in relationship, in the Church, in conclusions and it hasn't found security in any of those. Now
where do you find it? Is it out there? Or somewhere else?
We are learning together the futility of security in the projec-
tions of thought, whatever it is. I want to learn where to
find absolute security – if one has that, the whole problem
of fear ends, total fear, both physiological and psychological.

Our minds are active, chasing one thought after another.
Our minds in their movement of thought have gaps between
the thoughts, an interval, a time interval. And thought is
always trying to find a means where it can abide, abide in
the sense of hold. What thought creates, being fragmentary,
is total insecurity. I wonder if you see this? Therefore there
is complete security in being completely nothing – which
means not a thing created by thought. To be *absolutely
nothing*, means a total contradiction of everything you have
learnt, everything that thought has put together. To be not
a thing. If you are nothing you have complete security. It is
only in the becoming, wanting, desiring, pursuing that there
is insecurity.

So seeing the nature of time, which is the movement of thought, apart from chronological time; seeing the whole nature of fear as the movement of thought – as the achievement of an idea, or as living in the past, in the romantic, idiotic, sentimental past, or as living in knowledge, which is also fragmentary – we see that action is always fragmentary, never complete. Action means to act now, and that can only take place when there is complete security. The security that thought has created is no security. That is an absolute truth. And the absolute truth is when there is nothing, when you are nothing. You know what it means to be nothing? No ambition – which doesn't mean you vegetate – no competition, no aggression, no resistance, no barriers built by hurt. You are absolutely nothing. Then what happens to our relationships when we are nothing? You understand? Then what is it to be related to another? Have you ever thought about all this, or is it all tragically new?

Our relationship is never stable, and therefore it is a perpetual battle, perpetual division, each seeking his own pursuits, his own enjoyments, isolated. That relationship, being insecure, must inevitably bring division and therefore conflict – right? When in that relationship there is complete security there is no conflict. But you may be completely nothing, and I may not. If you are nothing, psychologically, inwardly; if you are completely secure because there is nothing, but I am still insecure, fighting, quarrelling, confused, what takes place? What is the relationship between you and me? Yours is not the certainty created by thought, not the certainty of the man who says, 'I believe in that,' and establishes his relationship in a belief, a conditioning, which breeds fear and therefore division. And that is going on all the time, you understand. Here it is entirely different. You have perceived, realized, understood, seen the truth that in this nothingness there is complete security. And I have not. What takes place between you and me? You have affection, love, compassion born of this tremendous unshakeable stability, and I, your friend, your wife, your husband, have not. What takes place? What will you do with me? Cajole me, talk to me, comfort me, tell me how stupid I am? What will you do?

Now, look at it differently. There are some 1,500 of us in this tent, and some of you, at least I hope so, have listened very carefully, given your attention, care, affection, and you realize that you are the world and the world is you – not verbally, but profoundly see the truth of it. You realize that and you see the immense and imminent responsibility to change radically because you have listened, not argued, held no opinion; you see the truth of it. And when there is that fundamental transformation, then what is your relationship to the world? It is the same question, you understand. What do you do? Do you wait for something to happen? If you wait for something to happen, then nothing will happen.

But if you actually see the truth that you are the world and the world is you, and you see the extraordinary importance of a basic transformation in yourself, then you affect the whole consciousness of the world – it is inevitable. And if you are completely, wholly secure – in the sense we are talking about – won't you affect me – I who am uncertain, despairing, clinging, attached – won't you affect me? Obviously you will. But the important thing is that you, listening, see the truth of this. Then it is yours, not something given to you by anyone else.

*From* BULLETIN 26, 1975

# Is There a Meaning to Life?

BROCKWOOD PARK, 5 SEPTEMBER, 1976

I think we ought to talk over together something that is of fundamental importance, which every human being should be involved in, because it concerns our life, our daily activity, the way we waste our days and years. What is it all about? What is it all for? We are born and we die, and during those years of pain and sorrow, joy and pleasure, there is the everlasting struggle and effort, going to the office or the factory for forty or fifty years, trying to climb the ladder of success, accumulating money, pleasure, experience, knowledge, and at the end death. Some scientists say that through knowledge comes the ascent of man. Is that so? We have an infinite amount of knowledge about many things – biological, archaeological, historical and so on – but apparently knowledge has not changed man radically, deeply; the same conflict, struggle, pain, pleasure, the everlasting battle for existence goes on.

Seeing all that continuing in every country and in every climate, what is it all about? It's very easy to reply with an emotional, romantic, neurotic explanation, or with an intellectual, rational explanation. But if you put all these aside as obviously being rather superficial, however intellectual, I think this is a very important question to ask – important to ask and to find an answer for oneself, not depending on some priest, some guru, or some philosophical concept, not asserting anything, not believing in anything, not having any ideal, but merely observing very deeply. Otherwise we lead a very mechanistic life. Our brains have become used to a mechanical way of life; part of this brain must be mechanical, necessarily so, in the acquisition of knowledge and the skilful use of that knowledge in every way of life, in every action outwardly, technologically. But this knowledge that one has acquired – and we can pile up knowledge more and more – does not answer the fundamental question: what is the meaning, the depth of our life?

One sees that there must be complete unity of mankind, because that is the only way the human race will survive physically, biologically. Politicians are not going to solve that problem – ever! On the contrary, they will maintain the divisions – it's very profitable. There must be unity of all mankind, it is essential for existence, but it cannot be brought about through legislation, through bureaucratic dogmas, laws and all the rest of it. So when one observes all this as a human being living in the chaos of a world that has almost gone mad – the selling of armaments for profit, killing people in the name of ideas, countries, God and so on – what is one to do? And what is it all for?

Religions have tried to offer the meaning of life – that is, organized, propagandistic, ritualistic religions. But, in spite of 2,000 or 10,000 years, man has merely asserted certain principles, certain ideals, certain conclusions, all verbal, superficial, non-realistic. So I think it becomes very important to discover a meaning for oneself, if one is at all serious – and one must be serious, otherwise one does not really live at all, which doesn't mean one never laughs or smiles – serious in the sense of a total commitment to the whole issue of life. So when we ask what is the meaning of life, we are faced with the fact that our brain is caught in a groove, caught in habit, in tradition, in the conditioning of our education, cultivating only knowledge, information, and so making it more and more mechanical.

If we are to inquire into this very deeply, there must be great doubt. Doubt, scepticism are essential, because they bring a certain quality of freedom of mind through negation of everything that man has put together – his religions, rituals, dogmas, beliefs which are all the movements of thought. Thought is a material process, as even the scientists accept. But thought has not solved our problems, it has not been able to delve deeply into itself; it has merely, being itself a fragment, broken up all existence into fragments. So there is this quality of the brain which is mechanistic, and necessarily so in certain areas, but inwardly, in the psychological structure of the human mind, there is no freedom. It is conditioned, it is bound by belief, by so-called ideals, by faith. So when one doubts all that, sets all that aside – not theoretically but factually, meticulously – then what is left? One is afraid to do that because one says to oneself, 'If I deny everything that thought has put together what is left?' When you realize the nature of thought – which is a mechanical process of time, measure, the response to memory, a process which brings more and more suffering, agony, anxiety and fear to mankind – and go beyond, negate it, then what is there?

To find out what there is we must begin with freedom, because freedom is the first and last step. Without freedom – not the freedom to choose – man is merely a machine. We think that through choice we are free, but choice exists only when the mind is confused. There is no choice when the mind is clear. When you see things very clearly without any distortion, without any illusions, then there is no choice. A mind that is choiceless is a free mind, but a mind that chooses and therefore establishes a series of conflicts and contradictions is never free because it is in itself confused, divided, broken up.

So to explore in any field there must be freedom, freedom to examine so that in that very examination there is no distortion. When there is distortion there is a motive behind that distortion, a motive to find an answer, a motive to achieve a desire, a solution to our problems, a motive which may be based on past experience, past knowledge – and all knowledge is the past. Wherever there is a motive there must be distortion. So can our mind be free of distortion?

And to examine our mind is to examine our common mind, because the content of our consciousness is the same as that of all human beings, who, wherever they live, go through the same process of fear, agony, torture, anxiety and endless conflict inwardly and outwardly. That's the common consciousness of mankind.

So when you examine your own consciousness, you are looking into the consciousness of man, and therefore it's not a personal, individualistic examination. On the contrary you are looking into the consciousness of the world – which is you. And this is a fact when you go into it very deeply. To have a mind that is free makes a tremendous demand; it demands that you as a human being are totally committed to the transformation of the content of consciousness, because the content makes the consciousness. And we are concerned with the transformation, with the total psychological revolution of this consciousness. To explore this you need great energy, an energy which comes into being when there is no dissipation of energy. One dissipates energy through trying to overcome 'what is', to deny or escape from 'what is', or to analyse 'what is', because the analyser is the analysed, the analyser is not different from that which he analyses. As we have said during these many talks for many years, this is a fundamental reality.

We are asking what is the meaning and the significance of life, and if there is any meaning at all. If you say there is, you have already committed yourself to something, therefore you cannot examine, you have already started with distortion. In the same way if you say there is no meaning to life, that is another form of distortion. So one must be completely free of both, the positive and the negative assertions. And this is the real beginning of meditation. The mushroom growth of gurus from India who are springing up all over the world has provided a great many meanings to that word. There is the transcendental meditation – and I wish they hadn't used that lovely word – which is the repetition of certain words – given at a certain price! – three times a day for twenty minutes. Constant repetition of any words will certainly give you a quality of quiet, because you have reduced the brain to a mechanical quietness. But that's no more transcendental than anything else. And through this we think we'll experience something that is beyond the material process of thought.

Man seeks experience other than the ordinary daily experience. We are bored, or fed up with all the experience we have had of life, and we hope to capture some experience which is not the product of thought. The word 'experience' means 'to go through', to go through with anything and end it, not remember it and carry it on. But we don't do that. To recognize an experience you must have already known it; it's not anything new. So a mind that demands experience, other than the mere physical, psychological experience, demands something far greater and above all this, will experience its own projection, and therefore it will still be mechanistic, materialistic, the product of thought. When you do not demand any experience, when you have understood the whole meaning of desire, which, as we have gone into many times, is sensation, plus thought and its image – then there is no distortion and illusion. Only then can the mind, the whole structure of consciousness being free, be capable of looking at itself without any distorting movement, without effort? Distortion takes place when there is effort – right? Effort implies 'me' and something I am going to achieve, division between me and that. Division invariably brings conflict. Meditation comes only when there is the complete ending of conflict. Therefore every form of meditation where there is effort, practice, control, has no meaning. Please don't accept what the speaker is saying. We are examining together, therefore it is important not to accept what is being said but to examine it for yourself.

So we must go into the question of control. We are educated from childhood to control – the whole process of controlling our feelings. In control there is the controller and the controlled, the controller who thinks he is different from that which he desires to control. So he has already divided himself, hence there is always conflict. That is, one fragment of thought says to itself, 'I must control other fragments of thought,' but the thought which says that is itself a part of thought. The controller is the controlled, the experiencer is the experienced, they are not two different entities or movements. The thinker is the thought; there is no thinker if there is no thought. This is very important because when this is realized completely, deeply, not verbally, not theoretically, but actually, then conflict comes to an end. When one realizes this profoundly as the truth, as a law, then all effort comes to an end, and meditation can only come into being when there is no effort of any kind.

It is necessary to meditate to find out if there is any meaning to life. And meditation is also laying the foundation of right conduct, right in the sense of accurate, not according to an ideal, not according to a pattern, not according to any formula, but action which takes place when there is complete observation of that which is going on in oneself. And through meditation we must establish right relationship between human beings, which means relationship without conflict. Conflict exists when there is division between the two images, which we have discussed a great deal, the image which you have of another and another has of you. And in meditation there must be no psychological fear whatsoever, and therefore the ending of sorrow, and there must be what we have previously talked about: compassion and love. That is the basis, the foundation of meditation. Without that you can sit cross-legged under a tree for the rest of your life, breathe properly – you know all the tricks one plays – none of these is going to help.

So when you have really, deeply, established a way of life

– which in itself is not an end, but only the beginning – then we can proceed to find out whether the mind, which is the totality, the brain, the entire consciousness, is quiet without any distortion. It is only when the mind is quiet, still, that you can hear properly. There are different kinds of silence: the silence between two noises, the silence between two thoughts, the silence after a long battle with oneself, the silence between two wars, which you call peace. All those silences are the product of noise. That is not silence. There is a silence which is not produced or cultivated, so that there is no 'me' to observe that silence, but only silence, quietness.

We began with the question: is there any meaning to life or none at all? In that silence you really don't ask that question; we have prepared the field of the mind that is capable of finding out. Yet we must find an answer. Where do we find the answer, and who is going to answer it? Am I, a human being, going to answer it? Or in that very silence is the answer? That is, when there is no distortion through motive, through effort, through a demand for experience, through the division between the observer and the observed, the thinker and the thought, there is no wastage of energy. Now in that silence there is that greater energy, and there must be that energy, that vitality, that strength to see beyond words. Because the word is not the thing, the description is not the described. To go to the moon, to create an instrument of a million parts, demands tremendous energy and the co-operation of 300,000 people to put the thing together. But that energy is totally different from the energy which we are talking about.

You see, the speaker is very serious about all this. He has spoken for fifty years and more on this, and as most minds are caught in grooves, deep or shallow, one is constantly watching to see if the brain forms a groove and feels secure in that groove and remains there, for if one stays in a groove, however beautiful, however pleasant, however comforting, then the mind becomes mechanical, repetitive, and so loses its depth, its beauty. So we are asking: is the silence mechanistic, a product of thought which says, 'There must be something beyond me, and to find that out I must be silent, I must control myself, I must subjugate everything to find out'? That is still the movement of thought, right? So we must understand the difference between concentration, awareness and attention.

Concentration implies the focusing of one's energy in a particular direction excluding all other directions, building a wall against all other things, resisting. Awareness is fairly simple – if you don't make it complicated. To be aware of everything around you, just to observe. Then there is attention. Attention implies that there is no centre from which you are attending. The centre is the 'me', and if you are aware from that centre, then your attention is limited. The centre exists when there is choice, and where there is choice there is always the 'me', my experience, my knowledge – me separate from you.

Now, what we are talking about is attention in which there is no centre at all. If you attend in that way now, as you are sitting there, you will see that your attention is vast, there is no boundary, so that your whole mind, everything, is completely attentive, without choice and therefore no centre, no 'me' who says, 'I am attentive.' In that attention there is silence, silence which contains the energy which is no longer dissipated. It is only such a mind that can find the answer, that can discover – unfortunately, if I describe it, it becomes unreal – something beyond all this travail, all this misery. If you give your whole energy, time, capacity to this, you no longer lead a shallow, meaningless life. And the whole of this is meditation, from the beginning to the end.

*From* BULLETIN 35, 1978

# A Quiet Mind

Have you ever noticed that our minds are rarely very quiet? We very rarely have a free mind, without any problems or, having problems, have only put them aside for a while. Have you ever had a mind that is not cluttered, is not stretching out, not seeking anything, but is absolutely silent and observing, not only what is happening in the world but also what is happening in the world of one's own inner existence of attitudes and travails – just observing? Or are you always seeking, searching, asking, analysing, demanding, trying to fulfil, trying to follow somebody, some ideal or other, or trying to establish a good relationship with another? Why is there this constant struggle and strife and seeking? You go to India seeking something extraordinary that you think is going to happen when you get there, following somebody who tells you to dance, to sing or to do whatever you want. There are those who try to force you to meditate in a certain fashion, to accept authority, to perform certain rituals, shout when you like and so on. Why are you doing all this? What is your everlasting thirst? What is it that you are seeking?

Remaining quietly in one's own home, or taking a solitary walk, can one ask why there is this everlasting thirst? We have talked about fear, and about sorrow and pleasure; we have also talked about intelligence, love and compassion. We pointed out that without intelligence there cannot be love or compassion. They go together. Not the intelligence of books, the cunning contrivance of thought, nor the intelligence of the very clever, subtle mind; but the intelligence that perceives directly what is false, what is dangerous; and perceiving, immediately lets it go. Such a quality of mind is intelligent.

Perhaps we could talk over together the nature of meditation and see if there is anything in life – not only in material activities and material possessions, money, sex, sensations, but beyond all that – that is really sacred, not put together by thought; actually, for ourselves, perhaps through meditation, being free of all illusion, deceit and thinking very honestly, find out if there is something sacred.

Most people have had varieties of experience, not only sensual experiences but incidents that have brought about various emotional, sensational and romantic movements. These experiences that one has had are rather trivial; perhaps all experiences are rather trivial. When one begins to inquire what it is that we are all seeking, wanting, longing for, is it not a superficial, mere sensory experience, something which desire seeks, which must obviously be rather superficial? Can we, in thinking this over together, move from the superficiality to a deeper, wider inquiry? That is, find out if all our longings are merely superficial and sensory; or is the longing, the searching, the thirst for something, far beyond all that?

How do you inquire into this? Through analysis? Analysis is still the same movement of thought, looking back. Analytically, thought examines itself and its own experiences; its examination is still limited because thought itself is limited. That is clear. But that is the only instrument we have and we keep on using the same instrument, knowing that it is limited, knowing that it cannot solve the problem or have the capacity to inquire very deeply. We never realize, I think, that this instrument, however sharp or however much used, cannot solve the problem. We do not seem to be capable of putting it aside.

Thought has created the technological world. Thought has created all the divisions in the world; not only the national divisions, but the religious divisions, the ideological divisions and every form of division between two people, however much they may think they love each other. That thought, in its activity, being limited, being the result of the past, must inevitably bring about division and therefore limitation. Thought can never see the whole. Is such activity superficial? Or can thought, with its limitation, inquire more deeply?

Is observation the instrument of thought? To observe: does that involve the movement of thought? You may observe, then conceive and create through that observation. That creation, arising from that observation, is the movement of thought. One sees a colour; there is the simple observation of it; then the reaction of like and dislike, prejudice and so on, the movement of thought. Can one observe without any movement of thought? Does that require a kind of discipline? Discipline: the root of that word is to learn. To learn; not to conform, not to imitate, not to make the mind dull in routine. Now, can one learn the activity of observation without thought creating images out of that observation and then acting according to those images? Can one merely observe? Which is to observe and to learn about, or to be aware of, the way the movement of thought interferes with observation. To learn about it. That is actual discipline, to learn.

When there is observation of, say, our longing or thirst for something, can one look without any motive, without the past, which is desire, or the conclusions of thought, interfering with the actual observation? Generally the purpose of learning is to accumulate knowledge, and from that to act, skilfully or unskilfully – it depends. Alternatively, you act and then learn, which is to accumulate knowledge from action. So our actions are always based upon the past, or on the past projecting the future and acting according to that projection.

Now, we are pointing out something entirely different from accumulating knowledge and then acting; something entirely different from one's actions being the result of the past or of the projection of the future, actions based on time – yesterday meeting the present, which is today, modifying itself and proceeding. One's action is normally based on that, so that our actions are always incomplete, obviously. In such action there are regrets, a sense of frustration, it is never complete.

Now we are pointing out something totally different: an observation in which the past and the future do not exist. Just to observe – as a good scientist does through a microscope – simply observing what is actually going on. When one observes what is actually going on, the thing which is observed undergoes a change. Can one observe the longing, the seeking, the urge? Has one the intense energy that is demanded just to observe without the movement of the past?

Observe what it is one wants in one's life, what it is one is seeking, longing for (most of you are seeking for something, otherwise you would not be here). One reads books on philosophy, psychology, or so-called religion. In religious books it is always pointed out that there is something beyond, something more and deeper. Having read those one might say, 'Perhaps there is, I am going after it.' Then one gets caught by the priests, by the gurus, by the latest fashion and so on. And one may think one has found something which is satisfying and one says, 'I am perfectly happy, I don't have to seek any more.' But it may perhaps be an illusion – most people like to live in illusions. And all your search and your demands and your hunger have not brought about a good society – a society that is based on peace, in which there is no violence.

The purpose of our inquiry into all this is to bring about a good society in which we human beings can live happily, without fear, without conflict, without all the striving, struggling and brutality. Society is built out of the relationship of people; if our relationship is not correct, precise, actual, then we create a society which is not sound; and that is what is happening in the world.

Why are human beings separate? You are seeking something, another is seeking something totally different; there is always this self-centred movement. The society which we have created is based on self-centred ambition, self-fulfilment and the self-centred discipline which says, 'I must', and which brings about violence. We are also inquiring into your mind. When we use the word 'mind', it is not your mind or my mind, but mind. Your mind is like the mind of thousands and millions of people – striving, struggling, demanding, following, accepting, obeying, idealizing, belonging to some religion, suffering sorrow, pain and anxiety; your mind is that and the other minds are like that. You may not see this, because your vanity, your sense of individual importance, may prevent this observation, which is actual. Human beings are similar psychologically; throughout the world they are so unhappy. They may pray, but prayer does not answer their problems; they are still unhappy, still striving, still despairing. This is the common mind. And so, when we are inquiring, we are inquiring into the human being, not just me and you – we are human beings.

Can one observe the outward world with its divisions, its terrors and dangers, and political criminalities, without drawing a conclusion? If we observe what is happening outwardly, and equally observe what is happening inwardly, then our actions are not your actions and my actions, because we have observed the same thing together.

Ask yourself what it is that you are seeking: is it money, is it security, is it to be free from fear so that you can have everlasting pleasure, is it that you are seeking to be free from the burden of sorrow – not only your own burden but the world's burden of sorrow – or are you seeking something which is timeless, something that thought has not touched at all, something essentially original, something that is absolutely incorruptible? Find out for yourself, as a human being, like the rest of human beings in the world, what it is that you are seeking, hungering after.

Are you seeking some new kind of experience because you have had experiences of various kinds and you have said, 'It is enough, I have had all those but I want some other kind' – something more, some experience which will give great delight, great understanding, an illumination, a transformation? How will you find out? To find out you must be free of all illusions. Which means complete honesty so that your mind does not deceive itself. Not to deceive yourself you must understand the whole nature of desire. Because it is desire that creates illusion – through desire one wants fulfilment, one hopes for something more. Unless you comprehend the whole nature and structure of desire, the mind will inevitably create illusion. Can your mind, having understood the activity of desire, know its relative value and therefore be free to observe? Which means you observe without any kind of illusion. Are you aware of illusions? When the mind is free of illusions, it is absolutely without any hypocrisy, clear and honest; then you can begin to inquire, inquire as to whether there is a timeless existence, a timeless truth. This is where meditation comes into being.

Probably you have played with meditation – transcendental meditation, Tibetan meditation, Hindu meditation, Buddhist meditation, Zen meditation – seriously or flippantly. As far as one can understand, the whole concept of these meditations is that thought must be controlled, that you must have discipline, you must subjugate your own feelings to something other than 'what is', through control, through constant alertness. Now, if you want to find out what meditation is, not just accepting what somebody says, then certain obvious things are necessary. There must be no authority, because then you depend, you struggle, you imitate and conform. Then one must understand the nature of control and who the controller is. From childhood we are trained, educated, to control or to suppress; or to go to the other extreme, which is what is happening nowadays, to do what you like, do your own thing! Is there a way of living without any form of control? Which does not mean doing what you like, indulging in permissiveness and so on. Is there a way of living in which there is not a shadow of control? To find that out you have to ask: who is the controller?

Who is the controller who says 'I must control my feelings' or 'I must allow my feelings to flow'? There is the controller and the thing to be controlled, so there is a division. Who is this controller? Is it not still the movement of thought? Thought has said, 'I have experienced this, I intend to do this,' which is the past; so the past *is* the controller. That which is happening now has to be controlled by the controller, which is the past.

I am not talking for my benefit. Although I have talked for fifty-two years I am not interested in talking. But I am interested to find out if you can also discover the same thing so that your own life will be totally different, transformed, so that you have no problems, no complexities, no strife or longing. That is the reason the speaker is talking, not for his own gratification, not for his own enjoyment, not for his own fulfilment.

So the controller is the result of thought, thought based upon knowledge, which is the past. Thought says, 'I must control what is happening now' – the actual. The actual is, for example, envy or jealousy – which you all know. Thought says, 'I must control it; I must analyse it; I must suppress it; or fulfil it.' So there is a division created by thought. In this there is deception, deception in the idea that the controller is different from that which is to be controlled. Both are created by thought. So the controller is the controlled. If you really understand this, go into this very seriously for yourself, you will see that the controller is unnecessary; only observation is necessary. When you observe, there is no controller or the controlled; there is just observing. Observe your envy, for example, observe it without naming it, without denying it or accepting it, just see the sensation, the reaction which arises, which has been called envy, and look at it without the word. Because the word represents the past. When you use the word 'envy' it strengthens the past.

There is a possibility of living without any sense of control. I am saying this not as a theory but as an actuality. The speaker says what he has done, not what he invents. There is a life without any sense of control and therefore no sense of conflict, no sense of division. That can only come into being when there is only pure observation. Do it and you will see. Test it out. When there is no conflict whatsoever, what takes place in the mind? Conflict implies movement; movement is time – time being from here to there, both physically and psychologically; the movement from one centre to another centre; or the movement from one periphery to another. There is this constant movement in our lives. Now if you observe this movement very carefully, what takes place in the mind?

You have understood the nature of thought, how it is limited knowledge which is stored up in the brain as memory, that memory acting as thought in action. You have understood how knowledge is always part of ignorance. So what takes place in the mind? The mind, as we have gone into it, is not only the capacity to think clearly, objectively, impersonally, but to see that it has the capacity to act not from thought but from pure observation. To observe what is actually taking place one must look without the response of the past shaping it. From that pure observation there is action. That is intelligence. And that is also the extraordinary thing called love and compassion.

So, the mind has this quality of intelligence and, naturally, with that intelligence goes compassion, love. Love is something other than mere sensation; it is totally unrelated to our demands and fulfilments and all the rest of it. So the mind now has this quality, this stability. It is like a rock in the midst of a stream, in the midst of a river, immovable. And that which is stable is silent. Do be absolutely clear about this. That clarity is stability; that clarity can then examine any problem. Without this clarity the mind is confused, contradictory, broken up; it is unstable, neurotic, seeking, striving, struggling. So we come to a point where the mind is totally clear and therefore completely immovable. Immovable, not in the sense of a mountain, but in the sense that it is completely without problems; therefore it is extraordinarily stable and yet pliable.

Now, such a mind is quiet. And you need to have a mind that is absolutely silent – absolutely, not relatively. There is the silence when you go of an evening into the woods; all the birds are still, the wind and the whisper of the leaves have ended; there is great outward stillness. And people observe this stillness and say, 'I must have that stillness,' and they depend on the stillness of being alone, being in solitude. But that is not stillness. Nor is the stillness created by thought which says, 'I must be still, I must be quiet, I mustn't chatter'. But that is not it, because that is the result of thought operating on noise. We are talking of a stillness which is not dependent on anything. It is only this quality of stillness, this absolute silence of the mind, that can see that which is eternal, timeless, nameless – which is meditation.

*From* BULLETIN 39, 1980

# The Ending of Sorrow is Love

We are going to cover a lot of ground this evening. Yesterday evening we were talking about sorrow and the ending of sorrow. With the ending of sorrow there is passion. Very few of us really understand or go deeply into the question of sorrow. Is it possible to end all sorrow? This has been a question which has been asked by all human beings, perhaps not very consciously, but deeply they have wanted to find out, as we all do, if there is an end to human suffering, human pain and sorrow. Because without the ending of sorrow there is no love.

Sorrow is a great shock to the nervous system, like a blow to the whole physiological as well as psychological being. And we generally try to escape from it by taking drugs, drinks and engaging in various forms of religious escapism; or we become cynical; or accept things as inevitable.

Can one go into this question very deeply, seriously? Is it possible not to escape from sorrow at all? Perhaps my son dies, and there is immense sorrow, shock, and I discover that I'm really a very lonely human being. I cannot face it, I cannot tolerate it, so I escape from it. And there are many escapes – religious, mundane or philosophical. Is it possible not to escape in any form from the ache, the pain of loneliness, the grief, the shock, but remain completely with the event, with this thing called suffering? Is it possible for you to hold any problem, hold it, not try to solve it, but to look at it as if you held a precious jewel, exquisitely handcrafted? The very beauty of the jewel is so attractive, so pleasurable, that we keep looking at it. In the same way if we could, without a movement of thought or escape, hold our sorrow, then that very action of not moving away from the fact brings out a total release from that which has caused pain.

We also wish to consider what beauty is – not the beauty of a person or the beauty of paintings and statues in museums or the most ancient endeavours of man to express his own feelings in stone or in paint or in a poem, but to ask ourselves what is beauty. Beauty may be truth. Beauty may be love. But without understanding the nature and the depth of that extraordinary word 'beauty', we may never be able to come upon that which is sacred. So we must go into the question of what is beauty.

What actually takes place when we see something greatly beautiful like the mountain full of snow against the blue sky? For a second, the very majesty of that mountain, the immensity of it, its lines against the blue sky, drive away all self-concern. At that second there is no 'me' watching it. The very greatness of that mountain has driven away, for a second, all self-concern. Surely one must have noticed this. Have you noticed a child with a toy? He's been naughty all day long – which is right – and you give him a toy; then, for the next hour, until he breaks it, he is extraordinarily quiet; the toy has absorbed his naughtiness; the toy has taken him over. Similarly, when we see something extraordinarily beautiful, that very beauty absorbs us. That is, there is beauty when there is no travail of the self, when there is no self-interest. Do you understand that? Without being absorbed or shaken by something extraordinarily beautiful like a mountain or a valley in deep shadow, without being taken over by the mountain, is it possible to understand beauty, to understand it without the self? Because where there is self there is no beauty; where there is self-interest there is no love; and love and beauty go together – they are not separate.

We ought also to talk over together what is death. This is one certain thing which we all have to face. Whether we are rich or poor, ignorant or full of erudition, young or old, death is certain for every human being; we are all going to die. And we have never been able to understand the nature of death; we are always frightened of dying, aren't we? To understand death, we must also inquire into what is living. Are we wasting our life, dissipating our energies in various forms, dissipating by specialized professions? You may be rich, you may have all kinds of faculties, you may be a specialist, a great scientist or businessman; you may have power, position, but at the end of life has all that been a waste? All this travail, all the sorrow, all the tremendous anxiety, insecurity, the foolish illusions that man has collected – his gods, all the saints and so on – has all that been a waste? Please, this is a serious question that one must ask oneself. Another cannot answer this question.

We have separated living from dying. Dying is at the end of one's life; we put it as far away as possible – a long interval of time; but we have, at the end of a long, long journey, to die. And what is it that we call living – earning money, going to the office from nine to five? And you have endless conflict, fear, anxiety, loneliness, despair, depression. This whole way of existence, which we call life, living – this enormous travail of man, his endless conflict, deception, corruption – is that living? This is what we call living; we know it; we are very familiar with it; it is our daily existence. And death means the ending of all that, the ending of all the things that we have thought, that we have accumulated, enjoyed. And we are attached to all this. We are attached to our family, to money, to knowledge, to the beliefs that we have lived with, to the ideals; we are attached to all that. And death says, 'That's the end of it, old boy.'

We are afraid of dying, which is letting go all the things we have known, all the things that we have experienced, gathered – the lovely furniture which we have and the beautiful collection of pictures. Death comes and says, 'You can't have any of those any more.' And we cling to the known, afraid of the unknown. We can invent reincarnation. But we haven't inquired what it is that is born in the next life.

Now the question is: why has the brain separated living and death? Why has this division taken place? Does this division exist when there is attachment? Can one live in the modern world with death – not suicide, we are not talking about that – but end all attachment, which is death, while one lives? I am attached to the house I am living in. I have bought it, paid a great deal of money for it, and I am attached to all the furniture, the pictures, the family, the memories of it all. And death comes and wipes all that out. So can you live every day of your lives with death, ending everything every day, ending all your attachments? For that's what it means to die. We have separated living from dying, therefore we are perpetually frightened. But when you bring life and death together – the living and the dying – then you will find that there is a state of the brain in which all knowledge as memory ends.

You need knowledge to write a letter, to come here, to speak English, to keep accounts, to go to your home and so on. Can the brain use knowledge when necessary yet be free of all knowledge? Our brain is recording all the time; you are recording what is being said now. That record becomes a memory, and that memory, that recording, is necessary in a certain area, the area of physical activity. So, can the brain use knowledge when necessary but be free of old knowledge? Can the brain be free so that it can function totally in a different dimension? That is, every day when you go to bed, wipe out everything that you have collected; die at the end of the day.

You hear a statement of this kind: living is dying; they are not two separate things at all. You hear that statement, not only with the hearing of the ear but, if you are listening carefully, you hear the truth of it, the actuality of it. And for the moment you see the clarity of it. So, is it possible for each one of us at the end of the day to die to everything that is not necessary, to every memory of hurt, to our beliefs, our fears, our anxieties, our sorrow; end all that every day? Then you find that you are living with death all the time, death being the ending.

One is attached to so many things – to one's guru, to accumulated knowledge, to money, to the beliefs one has lived with, to ideals, to the memory of one's son, daughter and so on. That memory is you; your whole brain is filled with memory, and you are attached to this whole consciousness. That is a fact. Then death comes and says, 'That's the end of your attachment.' And we are frightened, frightened of being completely free from all that, frightened of death, cutting off everything we have got. You can invent and say, 'I will continue in the next life,' but what is it that continues? Do you understand my question? What does that desire to continue mean? Is there a continuity at all, except of the things which are all brought together by thought?

Thought is limited and so creates conflict; we went into all that. And the self, the ego, the persona, is a bundle of complicated, ancient and modern memories. We live by memories. We live by knowledge, acquired or inherited, and that knowledge is what we are. The self is the knowledge of past experiences, thoughts and so on. The self is that. The self may invent that there is something divine in us, but that is still the activity of thought. And thought is always limited. You can see this for yourself, you don't have to study books and philosophies; you can see for yourself clearly that you are a bundle of memories. And death puts an end to all that memory. Therefore one is frightened. The question is: can one live in the modern world with death?

Then we ought to talk over together what is love. Is love sensation? Is love desire? Is love pleasurable? Is love put together by thought? Do you love your wife or husband or your children? Is love jealousy? Don't say no. Is love fear, anxiety, pain and all the rest of it? What is love? And without that quality, that perfume, that flame – you may be very rich, you may have a sense of power, position, importance – without love you are just an empty shell. So we ought to go into this question of love. If you loved your children, would there be wars? If you loved your children, would you allow them to kill others? Can love exist where there is ambition? Please face all this.

Love has nothing whatsoever to do with pleasure, with sensation. Love is not put together by thought; therefore it is not within the structure of the brain. It is something entirely outside the brain because the brain by its very nature, its structure, is an instrument of sensation, of nervous responses and so on. Love cannot exist where there is mere sensation. Memory is not love.

Also we should talk over together what is a religious life and what is religion. Again this is a very complex question. Human beings have sought something beyond the physical, beyond the everyday existence of pain, of sorrow or pleasure. They have sought something beyond, first in the clouds; the thunder was the voice of god. Then they worshipped trees, stones. Villagers far away from this ugly, beastly town still worship stones, trees, small images. Man wants to find out if there is something sacred, and the priest comes along and says, 'I will show you,' just as a guru does. The Western priest has his rituals, his repetitions, his fancy dress and worship of his particular image. And you – you have your own images. Or you don't believe in any of that; you say you are an atheist. But you and the speaker want to find out something that may be beyond time, beyond all thought. So we are together going to inquire, exercise our brain, our reason, our logic, to find out what is religion, what is a religious life, and if it is possible to live a religious life in this modern world.

So let us find out for ourselves what is really, truly a religious life. And that can only be found out when we understand what religions actually are and put aside all that – not belong to any religion, to any organization, to any guru, to any so-called spiritual authority. There is no spiritual authority whatsoever; that is one of the crimes that we have committed; we have invented a mediator between truth and ourselves.

When you begin to inquire into what is religion, you are living a religious life; not at the end of it. In the very process of looking, watching, discussing, doubting, questioning, having no beliefs, or faith, you are already leading a religious life. You are going to do that now.

You seem to lose all reason, all logic and sanity when it comes to religious matters. So we have to be logical, rational, doubting, questioning all the things that man has put together – the gods, the saviours, the gurus and their authority. That is not religion, that is merely the assumption of authority by the few. You give them authority. So set all that completely aside.

Have you ever noticed that where there is disorder socially, politically, in human relationships, there comes a dictator, a ruler? Where there is disorder in your own life you will create an authority; you are responsible for the authority and there are people who are too willing to accept that authority. Where there is fear, man inevitably seeks something that will protect him, that will hold him in a sense of security. And out of that fear we invent gods. Out of that fear we invent all the rituals, all the circus that goes on in the name of religion. All the temples in this country, all the churches and mosques, are put together by thought. You may say there is direct revelation. Doubt that revelation. You accept it, but if you use logic, reason, sanity, you will see the superstitions that you have accumulated; all that is not religion. Obviously. Can you put that aside to find out what is the nature of religion, what is the mind, the brain, that holds the quality of religious living? Can you as a human being who is frightened not invent, not create illusion, but face fear? Fear can completely disappear psychologically when you remain with it, not escape from it, but give your whole attention to it. It is like a light being thrown on fear, a great flashing light, and then that fear disappears completely. And when there is no fear, there is no god; there is no ritual; all that becomes unnecessary, stupid. The things that thought has invented become irreligious, because thought is merely a material process based on experience, knowledge, memory. Thought invents the whole rigmarole, the whole structure of organized religions which have lost completely all meaning. Can you put aside all that, voluntarily, not seeking a reward at the end of it? Will you do it? When you do, then there is nobody to ask what is religion.

Is there something beyond all time and thought? You may ask the question, but if thought invents something beyond, that is still a material process. Thought is a material process because it sustains knowledge in the brain cells. The speaker is not a scientist but you can watch it in yourself; you can watch the activity in your brain which is the activity of thought. So if you can put aside all that voluntarily, easily, without any resistance, then you will inevitably ask: is there something beyond all time and space? Is there something that has never been seen before by any man? Is there something immensely sacred? Is there something that the brain has never touched? So we are going to find out – that is, if you have taken the first step and wiped away all this rubbish called religion. Because you have used your brain, your logic, you doubt, you question.

Then, what is the meditation that is part of religion? What is meditation? To escape from the noise of the world, to have a silent mind, a quiet mind, a peaceful mind? For that you practise a system, a method, a mode, to become aware, to keep your thoughts under control. You sit crosslegged and you repeat some mantra. You repeat, repeat, repeat and carry on with your self-interested way, your egotistic way, and the mantra has lost its meaning.

So what is meditation? Is meditation a conscious effort? You meditate consciously, practise in order to achieve something – to achieve a quiet mind, brain, to achieve a sense of stimulus of the brain. What is the difference between that meditator and the man who says, 'I want money, so I work for it'? What is the difference between the two? Both are seeking an achievement. One is called spiritual achievement, the other is called mundane achievement – they are both in the line of achievement. To the speaker, that is not meditation at all; any conscious, deliberate, active desire with its will is not meditation.

So, one has to ask if there is meditation that is not brought about by thought. Is there meditation of which you are not aware? Do you understand all this? Any deliberate process of meditation is not meditation. That is so obvious. You can sit cross-legged for the rest of your life, breathe and all the rest of that business, and you will not come anywhere near the other thing, because that is a deliberate action to achieve a result – the cause and the effect. But the effect becomes the cause; so you are caught in a cycle. Is there a meditation that is not put together by desire, by will, by effort? The speaker says there is. You don't have to believe it; on the contrary you must doubt it, you must question it, as the speaker has questioned it, doubted it, torn it apart. Is there a meditation that is not contrived, organized? To go into that one must understand the brain which is conditioned, the brain which is limited, that brain which is trying to comprehend the limitless, the immeasurable, the timeless, if there is such a thing as the timeless. And for that it is important to understand sound. Sound and silence go together.

We have separated sound from silence. Sound is the world; sound is your heart beating; the universe is filled with sound; all the heavens, the million stars, the whole sky, are filled with sound. And we have made that sound into something intolerable. But when you listen to sound, the very listening is the silence; silence and sound are not separate. So meditation is something that is not contrived, organized. Meditation *is*. It begins with the first step, which is to be free of all your psychological hurts, to be free of all your accumulated fears, anxiety, loneliness, despair, sorrow. That is the foundation, that is the first step, *and the first step is the last step*. If you take that first step, it is over. But we are unwilling to take that first step because we don't want to be free. We want to depend – depend on power, on other people, on the environment, on our experience and knowledge. We are never free of all dependence, all fear.

The ending of sorrow is love. Where there is that love there is compassion. And that compassion has its own integral intelligence. And when that intelligence acts, that action is always true. There is no conflict where there is that intelligence. You have heard all this: you have heard of the ending of fear, the ending of sorrow; you have heard of beauty and love. But hearing is one thing and action is another. You hear all these things which are true, logical, sane, rational, but you won't act according to that. You go home and begin all over again with your worries, your conflicts, your miseries. So one asks: what is the point of it all? What is the point of listening to this speaker and not living it? The listening and not doing is the wastage of your life; if you listen to something that is true and not act, you are wasting your life. And life is much too precious – it is the only thing that we have. And we have also lost touch with nature, which means we have lost touch with ourselves, who are part of nature. We don't love trees, the birds, the waters and the mountains; we are destroying the earth; and we are destroying each other. And all that is such a waste of life.

When one realizes all this, not merely intellectually or verbally, then one lives a religious life. To put on a loincloth or to go begging or to join a monastery is not a religious life. A religious life begins when there is no conflict, when there is the sense of love not given only to one person and therefore restricted. So, there is, if you give your heart and mind and brain, something that is beyond all time. And there is the benediction of that – not in temples, not in churches, not in mosques. That benediction is where you are.

*From* BULLETIN 54, 1989

# Beauty, Sorrow and Love

OJAI, CALIFORNIA, 18 MAY 1985

What is it that human beings throughout the world have sought beyond their daily troublesome, boring and lonely lives? What is there beyond, not only for the individual but for the whole of humanity? What is there that is not touched by thought, that has no name, that may be eternal, lasting, enduring? We are going to talk over these matters and about meditation and yoga. Everybody seems to be interested in yoga – they want to keep young and beautiful.

Yoga has now become a business affair like everything else. There are teachers of yoga all over the world. And they are coining money – as usual. Yet yoga, at one time – I've been told by those who know a great deal about this – was only taught to the very, very few. Yoga does not mean merely to keep your body healthy, normal, active and intelligent. It also means – the word 'yoga' in Sanskrit means 'join together' – joining the higher and the lower; that is the tradition. There are various forms of yoga of which the highest form is called raja yoga – the king of yogas. That way of living was concerned not merely with physical well-being, but also, and much more, with the psyche. There was no discipline, no system, nothing to be repeated day after day. It was to have a brain that was in order, that was all the time active, but not chattering – active. It was to have a very deeply ordered moral, ethical and disciplined life, not based on the taking of various vows. Thereby, although the body was kept healthy, it was not of primary importance. What was of primary importance was to have a brain, a mind, a state of well-being, that was clear, active; not active in the sense of physical movement, but a brain in itself active, alive, full of vitality. But now yoga has become rather shallow, a source of profit, mediocre.

The highest yoga is not to be taught to the casual; it is something that you do, perhaps every day, to have perfect awareness of your body. You watch your body so that it does not make any movement, any gesture, which is not observed. There is no unnecessary movement of the body, but it is not controlled. Perhaps you may consider yoga to be something to be practised day after day to develop your muscles, to have a muscular body. It is not that at all. It is something you live all day long, watchfully observing, being clear about.

We were talking the other day about our relationship to nature, to all the beauty of the world, to the mountains, to the groves and to the hills and the shadows, the lakes and the rivers. We talked about the image made by thought which comes between oneself and the mountain, the fields and the flowers, just as one makes an image about one's wife or husband and so on; that image prevents complete relationship.

There is a relationship, between you and the speaker now. That relationship is very important to understand. The speaker is not persuading you to any point of view nor exerting any kind of pressure, so that you listen, accept or deny. He has no authority. He is not a guru. He has an abomination of the idea of leadership, psychologically or spiritually. It is an abhorrence to him – and he really means it. It is not something to be taken lightly.

The conversations we have had have been carried on mutually. They are not one-sided conversations. The world is peopled with bullies, the religious bullies, the newspapers, the politicians, the gurus and priests, the bullies in the family. Those bullies make us feel guilty; they attack first and you have to defend. That is the game that goes on in our relationship and it brings about a feeling of guilt.

We have talked about fear and why human beings, who

have evolved through many millennia, live with this terrible burden called fear. Fear is a sensation. Sensation takes many forms, the sensation of drugs, alcohol and so on, the sensation of sexuality, the sensation of achieving something, climbing the ladder, either a mundane ladder or the, so-called, spiritual ladder. We have many, many fears, which not only destroy the human capacity, but distort the brain, which distort or curtail or limit both our biological and psychological activity. We went into it. We said the root of fear is time and thought.

You can listen to this casually or seriously, as you listen to each other's conversation. But the words are not the thing. Fear is not the word; but the word may create the fear. The word is the picture, the idea. But the fact of fear is quite different. So one has to be clear as to whether the word is inducing or cultivating fear. Then the overcoming of that fear means overcoming the word, but not the fact.

And again one said how you face the fact is all-important: not the fact itself, but how you approach it, how you come to it. If one comes to fear with conclusions, with concepts of how to get over it, how to suppress it, or how to transcend it, if one goes to somebody to help overcome it, then that fear will continue in one form or another. And out of fear mankind has done terrible things. Out of fear of not having security we have destroyed human beings by the million. The last war and the previous war showed it; and where there is fear, there is God and all the comfort derived out of illusions. But when there is psychological security and therefore security biologically, there is freedom from fear. It is not physical security first and then psychological security after. The socialists and the totalitarians have tried to establish order outside and they are not succeeding. They are only suppressing. But if one starts to understand the whole psychological structure of oneself, of every human being, then one begins to understand the nature of fear; and it can be ended.

As it is such a beautiful morning, we ought to inquire together into beauty. What is beauty? If one may ask respectfully, what is your response to that question: what is beauty? Is it in the mountains and the shadows, in the dappled light under these trees? Is it a sheet of still water in the moonlight or the stars of a clear evening? Or the beautiful face, well-proportioned, having that inward beauty? Or does it lie in the pictures and statues in the museums? There is a marvellous statue in the Louvre, the *Victory of Samothrace*. Is that beauty? Or a beautiful woman, carefully made up; is that beauty?

One should ask this question of oneself because we are seeking this thing all the time. That is why museums have become so important. Is it because, in ourselves, we are so ugly, so broken up and fragmented that we can never see anything whole? We never live in a holistic way and so we think beauty is out there, in a picture, in a lovely poem of Keats, or in marvellously written literature.

So what is beauty? Is beauty love? Is beauty pleasure? Is beauty something that gives you *élan*, a sensation? When you see those hills behind there and the blue sky and the line of those mountains against the sky and the shadows and the sunburned grass and the shady trees, or see high peaks with their eternal snow, with a sky that has never been polluted, when you see these things, when you look at them, not verbalizing immediately, then what takes place? Does not the majesty of that mountain, the enormous solidity of it, at that second when you see it, drive away all your pettiness, all your worries and problems and all the travail of life? For that second you become silent.

It is like a small child who has been running about all day shouting and being a little naughty. What happens to that naughtiness when you give it a lovely, complicated toy? Its whole energy becomes concentrated in that toy and it is no longer naughty. That toy absorbs him; it becomes all-important. The child loves it and holds it – you have seen teddy bears worn out. And the mountain absorbs you for a second and you forget yourself. If you see a marvellous statue – not only one of the Grecian statues, but the ancient Egyptian ones with their extraordinary sense of earth, richness, stability and dignity – for a moment its dignity and immensity drive our pettiness away. Similarly, we adults are absorbed by toys, maybe it is our business, our chicanery in politics and so on. These things absorb us and if they are taken away, then we get depressed and from that we try to escape by running away from what we are.

So is not beauty something that takes place when 'you' are not; 'you' with all your problems, with your insecurity, and anxiety as to whether you are loved or not loved? When 'you' with all these psychological complexities are not, then that state is beauty. When 'you' are not, there is beauty which is not pleasure, nor is it sensation.

Pleasure, for us, is an extraordinarily important thing; the pleasure of a sunset, the pleasure of seeing somebody whom you like enjoying himself. So we ought to talk over together the whole concept of pleasure, because pleasure is what we want, if we are honest. And that is our difficulty, for we are never seriously honest with ourselves. We think that to be so honest with ourselves may lead to trouble, not only for ourselves but for others.

What is pleasure? To possess a beautiful car, or have lovely old furniture, to polish, to look at, to evaluate? Then one identifies oneself with that furniture; then one becomes that furniture, because whatever one identifies oneself with, one is that. It may be an image, it may be a piece of furniture, it may be some idea, some conclusion, some ideology, and the identification is something which is convenient, satisfying; it does not give too much discomfort and brings us a great deal of pleasure. Yet pleasure goes with fear. I do not know if you have watched it.

It is the other side of the coin, but one does not want to look at the other side, saying to oneself that pleasure is the most important thing, even through drugs, which are being taken more and more throughout the world. And there is pleasure in possessing a woman or a man, the pleasure of power over somebody, over wife or husband. We admire power; we extol power; we idolize power, whether it is the spiritual power of the religious hierarchy, or the power of a politician, or the power of money. To the speaker, power is evil. There are those who want power, through knowledge, through enlightenment. (There is enlightenment, but not of the kind of stupid nonsense they talk about which gives them power.) Education, television, the environment, are all making us mediocre. We read too much about what other people are saying. And success – success is utter mediocrity.

Because we ourselves lack power, position, status, we hand it over to somebody else and then worship it, adore it. And we have lived that way for millennia, seeking power, security, money, and feeling that they will give freedom; which is not freedom at all. In that freedom you can choose what you want or what you like; but is that freedom? Have you gone into this question of what real freedom means? Not in heaven? (You remember that joke – may I repeat it? Two men are in heaven with wings and haloes. One says to the other, 'If I am dead, why do I feel so awful?') So all forms of pleasure are part of our lives, which become more and more sensational, more easy, vulgar and mediocre. And so we go on with our pleasures and in their wake comes fear.

The word 'sensation' means 'the activity of the senses'. The activity of the senses is always partial, limited, unless all the senses are fully awakened. You want more and more, for the past sensation has not been sufficient. Is there a holistic activity for all the senses? Our sensations are limited and you take drugs and so on to have greater sensations. But they are still limited and you are asking for more. When you ask for more, it is because your sensations are partial. So I am asking: is there a holistic awareness of all the senses – so that there is never an asking for more? And where there is this complete awareness of all the senses – not that 'one' is aware of it – but an awareness of the senses in themselves, then there is no centre from which there is an awareness of that wholeness. When you look at those hills, can you look at them not only with your eyes – the optic nerves operating – but with all the senses, with all your energy, with all your attention? Then there is no 'me' at all. When there is no 'me', there is no asking for more, or trying to achieve something greater.

All these matters we have spoken about are related to each other. Guilt, the psychological wounds which most people have, and the consequences of those psychological wounds. The vanity of one's own cultivated intelligence and the images that one has built about oneself, it is they that get hurt – nothing else. Relationship, fear and pleasure; they are all interrelated; they are not something to be taken bit by bit, or separately, saying 'This is my problem' or 'If I can solve that, I do not mind the rest'. But the rest remains there. So can one see this movement as a whole, not just one partial movement at a time?

Sorrow is an immense subject. Sorrow has been in the minds of men and women from the beginning of time – sorrow which has never ended. If you travel, especially in the Asiatic world, or in Africa, you see immense poverty – immense! And you shed tears or do some social reforming, or give food or clothes, but there is still sorrow. And there is the sorrow for someone whom you have lost. You have their picture on the mantelpiece, or hung on the wall, you look at it and it revives all the memories connected with that picture and you shed tears. One sustains, nourishes, continues in loyalty, through that picture. That picture is not the person; nor are the memories; but we cling to those memories which give us more and more sorrow. There is the sorrow of those people who have very little in their lives, no money and only a few sticks of furniture. They live in ignorance; not the ignorance of something great, but the simple ignorance of their daily lives, of their having nothing inside them – not that the rich people have either; they have it in the bank account, but nothing inside. Then there is the immense sorrow of mankind, which is war. Millions have been killed; you have seen in Europe thousands of crosses, all in straight lines. How many women, men, children, have cried in every community, every country, every state. Throughout historical times there have been wars every year – tribal wars, national wars, ideological wars, religious wars. In the Middle Ages they tortured people considered heretics. From the beginning of man, sorrow has continued in different forms. Sorrow of poverty, the poverty of not being able to fulfil your desires, the poverty of achievement, for there is always more to be achieved; all of which has brought immense sorrow – not only personal sorrow, but the sorrow of humanity. In the totalitarian states, we read about what is happening, but never shed a tear. We are indifferent to it all, because we are so consumed by our own sorrow, our own loneliness, our own inadequacy. So we ask ourselves, is there an ending to sorrow? Is there an ending to our personal sorrows, with all the implications of that ending? If we are at all seriously involved, committed to find out, is there an end to sorrow? And if there is an end, what is there then – because we always want a reward: if we end this, we must have that? We never end anything for itself *per se*.

What is the relationship of sorrow to love? One knows what sorrow is – great pain, grief, loneliness, sense of isolation. One's sorrow is felt to be entirely different from another's, and in the very feeling of it one has become isolated. We know, not only verbally, but in depth, in the inward feeling of our very being what the meaning of that sorrow is. And what is the relationship of sorrow to love? What is love? Have you ever asked this question of yourself? Is it sexual sensation, the reading of a lovely poem, looking at these marvellous old trees? Is love pleasure? Please – we must be very honest with ourselves, otherwise there is no fun in this. (Humour is necessary: to be able to laugh, to be able to laugh together at a good joke, not when you are by yourself, but together.) We are asking ourselves, what is love? Is love desire? Is love thought? Is love something that you hold and possess? Is love that which you have when you worship the statue, the image, the symbol? Is that love? The symbol, the statue or the picture, is the result of thought. Your prayers are put together by thought. Is that love? Of course, fear is obviously not love. Have you ever looked at hate? If you hate, you dispel fear. If you really hate somebody, there is no fear. Through complete negation in oneself of what is not love, totally putting aside all that which is not love, then that perfume is there. That perfume can never go once you have put aside completely those things which are not love. Then love, which goes with compassion, has its own intelligence, which is not the intelligence of the scientific brain. When one has that love, that compassion, there is no grief, no pain, no sorrow. That love is there when you negate everything that is not love. If there is love, then you will never kill another – never! You will never kill an animal for your food. (Of course, go on eating meat, I am not telling you not to.) It is an immense thing to come upon it. Nobody can give it to another. Nothing can give it to you. But, if you, in your being, put aside all that which is not love, all that which thought has put together, then you are really renewed, with all your problems totally emptied, then the other thing is. It is the most positive thing, the most practical thing. The most impractical thing in life is to build armaments, to kill people, is it not? That is what your tax money is being spent on. I am not a politician, so do not listen to all this. But see what we are doing, and what we are doing is the society which we have created. Society is not different from us, we have formed it. Love has nothing to do with any organization, or with any person. Like a cool breeze from the ocean, you can shut it out or live with it. When you live with it, it is something totally different. There is no path to it; there is no path to truth – no path whatsoever. One has to live with it. One can only come to it when one has understood the whole psychological nature and structure of oneself.

Tomorrow we ought to talk about death. It is not a morbid subject. It is not something to be avoided. If you have lived the thing that we have been talking about, you will come to all this delicately, gently, quietly, not out of curiosity. You will come to it hesitantly, with great dignity, with inward respect. Like birth, it is a tremendous thing. Death also implies creation – not invention. Scientists are inventing; their invention is born from knowledge. Creation is continuous. It has no beginning and no end. It is not born out of knowledge. And death may be the meaning of creation – not a matter of having a next life with better opportunities, a better house, better refrigerator. It may be a sense of tremendous creation, endlessly, without beginning and end.

*From* BULLETIN 51, 1986